The Easy Paleo Diet Beginner's Guide

Quick Start Diet and Lifestyle Plan PLUS 74 Satisfying Recipes

Andrea Huffington

NaturalWay Publishing

Atlanta, Georgia USA

ISBN 978-1-491010-47-1

All Rights Reserved

Readers' Feedback

"I did not realise the impact food has on how we think and feel until I read this book. I'm changing the way I eat now, and I can feel the change inside me already. I am so thankful."

★★★★☆ **Leah Werfel - Germany**

"Superb. Well written. This little book packs a punch and makes it simple and easy to go the paleo route amidst a sea of temptation."

★★★★★ **Donald N. Parkhurst - Idaho**

"My brother had me read this book, now I'm telling all my friends about it too. This book will give me the edge I need for college next year."

★★★★☆ **Elizabeth J. Irish - Florida**

Thank you for downloading my book. Please REVIEW this book on Amazon. I need your feedback to make the next version better. Thank you so much!

Books by Andrea Huffington

Paleo Slow Cooker Recipes

The Easy Paleo Diet Beginner's Guide

Going Paleo on a Budget

www.amazon.com/author/andrea-huffington

The Paleo Diet Made Simple

Did you ever stop to think that perhaps when it comes to nature and our bodies our ancient ancestors knew more than we do? And I don't mean about the science of it all, I'm talking about the life experiences that not only shaped their lives but also those of generations to come.

People have a tendency to put things into boxes; "this is good", they say, or "this is bad". However, not many of them stop to think that what's good for one person is not necessarily good for another, and what's healthy for you is not actually healthy for me. It's all about perceptions at the end of the day, and one of them dictates that avoiding eating some foods is good for you, while it could be the opposite.

My book comes to challenge some of these perceptions by explaining how a Paleo diet can prove useful to a modern person's health. It gives the readers the full picture about its subject, offers advice, proposes training exercises, and tells them what they need to do to lose weight and regain their health, without sacrificing too much. "Return to the basics"; that's my philosophy one could say. And I can guarantee that these *basics* can change your life for the better forever.

TABLE OF CONTENTS

Disclaimer

While all attempts have been made to provide effective, verifiable information in this Book, neither the Author nor Publisher assumes any responsibility for errors, inaccuracies, or omissions. Any slights of people or organizations are unintentional.

This Book is not a source of medical information, and it should not be regarded as such. This publication is designed to provide accurate and authoritative information in regard to the subject matter covered. It is sold with the understanding that the publisher is not engaged in rendering a medical service. As with any medical advice, the reader is strongly encouraged to seek professional medical advice before taking action.

Introduction

The Paleo diet is sometimes referred to as the "Primal" diet in reference to author Mark Sisson's *Primal Blueprint* method of choosing and preparing foods. There are many similarities in the diet plans and the terms can essentially be used interchangeably. The key differences are that a Primal diet plan generally contains dairy foods and an almost unlimited intake of saturated fats, whereas a Paleo diet plan generally avoids dairy products and restricts the overall saturated fat intake.

Going Paleo or going Primal essentially means going back to eating in a way that closely resembles the way our "caveman" ancestors ate, and making the same sort of food choices that not only allowed them to survive but also to thrive. Our modern-day lifestyles of highly processed foods and high stress levels have led to an increase in modern-day diseases and potentially life threatening health issues that are largely avoidable by simply addressing our daily diet and gaining an understanding of how what we eat, when we eat, and the way we eat impacts our bodies.

Contrary to many overly complicated weight-loss and exercise plans, the key to losing unwanted body fat and gaining a lean, energized, healthy physique is to keep things simple. The following chapters are designed to provide you with the knowledge and understanding you need to stock your pantry and refrigerator with healthy Paleo food choices, not only making it quick and simple to shop but also to prepare healthy meals easily by having everything you need available. The exercise plans provided give you the essential "need-to-know" information in terms of maximizing your efforts and promoting on-going fat loss, and they demonstrate just how simple it is to create practical workouts to suit any lifestyle without the need to join an expensive gym.

Chapter One: What is the Paleo Diet?

"The Paleo Diet as it has come to be known is simplicity itself. Limit your purchases at the supermarket to the outside aisles (produce, seafood, meat) and you are about 85 percent of the way there." – Dr Loren Cordain, founder of the Paleo Movement

The popularly used term "Paleo" is an abbreviation of Paleolithic, referring to the Paleolithic Era of around 2.5 million years ago. The Paleo diet is therefore based on eating the foods that would have been available to our Paleolithic or "caveman" ancestors and avoiding all forms of modern foods that would have been unavailable to hunter-gatherers of that time. In a nutshell, it's a healthy eating diet that focuses on eating good quality natural foods and cutting out unhealthy processed foods that have little or no nutritional value. The foods included in a Paleo diet are the ancient foods our bodies were designed to be able to digest easily while "on the move" and the foods avoided are those that only came into our diet as a result of modern-day farming practices.

However, it's worth noting that there are many Paleo diet variations and there is no one definitive diet in terms of what should or should not be included. Our "caveman" ancestors survived on the foods that were readily available to them and availability was, of course, determined by location. It's a common misconception that a Paleo diet is a low-carb diet, but while some hunter-gatherer groups would have lived on a diet of low-carb foods, other groups in different locations would have had easy access to high-carb foods such as coconuts, tubers and fish.

Where you live will inevitably influence your food choices when choosing to live a Paleo lifestyle. Sourcing good quality, *locally* grown produce is at the heart of any Paleo-based diet and eating the best produce available in your area in terms of both accessibility and affordability is an important element of adhering to a hunter-gatherer lifestyle.

Paleo made simple key point # 1:

If it's processed or packaged, it's probably not Paleo!

A Paleo diet is generally higher in daily protein and fat intake and lower in carbohydrate intake than the current figures promoted by the U.S. Department of Agriculture (USDA) in its current healthy eating guidelines. According to the USDA, a balanced daily diet should consist of 60 percent carbohydrates, 30 percent fats, and 10 percent protein, but a Paleo-based diet generally includes a higher percentage of protein and "healthy" fat (including saturated fats considered "unhealthy" by USDA standards) and therefore a lower percentage of carbohydrates. Paleo sources of protein are lean meats, preferably from grass-fed animals, and sources of "healthy" fats in the form of omega-3 essential fatty acids are found in fish. The USDA promotes whole grains and starchy foods such as bread, pasta and potatoes as the main sources of carbohydrates in a balanced diet but the main sources of carbohydrates in a Paleo diet are fruits and vegetables, ensuring you also consume a rich source of health-promoting micro-nutrients in the form of vitamins and minerals.

By avoiding all processed and packaged foods, and by cutting grains and other modern farmed foods from your diet, you create a daily diet of foods that would be instantly recognizable as foods to our hunter-gatherer ancestors, and that's essentially what going "Primal" is all about. As Dr. Cordain, the founder of the Paleo diet says, it's all about "eating the foods to which we are genetically adapted."

Primal Blueprint Food Pyramid

For effortless weight loss, vibrant health, and maximum longevity

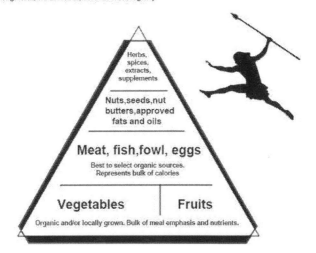

Herbs, spices, extracts, supplements

Nuts,seeds,nut butters,approved fats and oils

Meat, fish,fowl, eggs

Best to select organic sources.
Represents bulk of calories

Vegetables | Fruits

Organic and/or locally grown. Bulk of meal emphasis and nutrients.

Chapter Two: Why Go "Primal"?

"Live long. Drop dead" – Primal Blueprint slogan

There are many health benefits associated with adopting the eating and lifestyle practices of our "caveman" ancestors, not least the reduced risk of developing cardiovascular disease and weight related health concerns such as high blood pressure and type 2 diabetes. Taking steps to incorporate the ancient ways of Paleolithic times into modern life can bring the following:

- Increased energy – sugar induced "highs" and "lows" are replaced with an all-day energy balance. Fruits and vegetables provide a slow and steady release of energy which keeps you feeling physically and mentally "ready for action" throughout the day.
- Improved mental clarity and a more positive outlook on life in general.
- More restful sleep – also helping to boost your energy levels and your mood.
- Clearer skin – an improvement in overall complexion and often complete eradication of on-going skin conditions such as acne.
- Reduced allergies – symptoms of conditions such as eczema and asthma can be greatly alleviated.
- Reduced body fat stores – by increasing your fat intake and decreasing your carbohydrate intake, your body learns to burn fat for fuel. A diet high in carbs leads to raised insulin levels, which in turn causes your body to store fat. When fat is being stored, your body "craves" more carbs for fuel ... but more carbs leads to more fat storage! An added bonus of eating Paleo foods is that as your body adapts to burning fat as its main fuel source, your workouts become much more efficient

and long cardio sessions are no longer needed to help you get the lean, non-flabby physique you want.

Positive Benefits of Going Primal

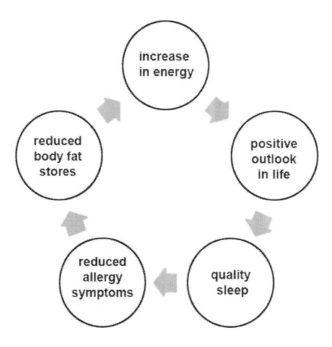

Removing processed foods from your daily diet removes a plethora of unnatural added ingredients such as preservatives, artificial colors and stabilizers that are scientifically linked to poor health concerns and food allergies. Less than 1 percent of the U.S. population has a true wheat allergy but it is thought that as many as 20 percent suffer from some form of wheat intolerance, highlighting the Paleo principle that our bodies are not genetically geared to eat and digest grains. The toxic properties of wheat, barley and rye grains are linked to the worldwide increase in obesity and the prevalence of diet related conditions such as gluten sensitivity, with National Institutes of Health statistics estimating that around 10 percent of the global population is currently suffering symptoms and that numbers are steadily growing.

Primal Proof Positive!

There are a huge number of inspirational transformation stories all over the internet, including many that tell of "miraculous" changes in physical and mental health as a result of switching to a Paleo-based diet.

Asthma – Shannon, a U.S. based personal trainer and CrossFit instructor has commented on many Paleo related forums that she has seen remarkable improvements in her clients who choose to switch to a Paleo lifestyle, not only in terms of fat loss but also in terms of athletic performance. Many of her clients have initially relied heavily on inhalers to help them cope with the symptoms of exercise-induced asthma but after only a few weeks of Paleo eating, they are able to participate in exercise sessions without using an inhaler at all.

Acne – Penny from the U.K. is one of many Paleo "success stories" in that her 35 year battle with acne finally ended after only a few weeks of following a Paleo-based diet. Coping with acne at any stage of life can be emotionally challenging and for many teenagers it leads to long-term psychological as well as physical scarring. The realization that a simple dietary change was all that was needed to turn her life around permanently *and* provide the added bonus of effortlessly shedding a few unwanted pounds has given her a new lease of life!

Weight Loss – Katie from Chicago is just one of many thousands of successful "dieters" who report finding the transition to eating a Paleo-based diet so easy that it does not feel like a "diet" at all. The ease of the transition made *staying* on the Paleo diet a lifestyle choice for Katie that's no longer about weight loss but all about looking great and feeling great – both internally and externally.

Chapter Three: Paleo Foods

"Red meat is not bad for you. Now blue-green meat, that's bad for you!" –
Tommy Smothers

Obviously, the world has changed almost beyond recognition over
the past 2.5 million years but the modern-day foods that most closely
resemble the foods available to our Paleolithic ancestors include the
following:

- **Grass-produced meat** – locally produced, grass-fed and
  organic sources are preferable to grain-fed sources. Offal is
  also included in a Paleo diet.
- **Fowl** – this includes game birds where available along with
  organically produced chicken, turkey and duck. Any wild meat
  or fowl must come from sustainable sources.
- **Fish** – wild varieties of fish, provided they come from
  sustainable sources, are preferable to farmed varieties as
  farmed fish often contains high levels of toxins such as
  mercury.
- **Seafood** – including shrimps, clams, lobsters, oysters, scallops
  and crab but it's important to consider the sustainability of
  the source.
- **Eggs** – organic, pasture-fed and free-range eggs are best but
  omega-3 enriched eggs provide a suitable alternative in areas
  where pastured eggs are unavailable.
- **Vegetables** – virtually all varieties are acceptable but those
  with relatively high starch contents such as potatoes and
  squashes should be eaten in moderation compared to lower
  starch varieties such as broccoli, asparagus, avocado and
  cabbage.
- **Oils** – Paleo experts disagree on the best types of oil but the
  general consensus is that natural sources such as grass-fed
  butter, tallow, ghee, avocado oil, macadamia oil, walnut oil,

flaxseed oil, coconut oil and olive oil are best for cooking and that any form of processed oil should be used sparingly for dressings only and not for cooking.

- **Fruits** – all fruits can be eaten in moderation with vegetables making up the bulk of the carbohydrate intake on a Paleo diet. The preferred choice is to eat any locally grown type of berry when in season.
- **Nuts** – all types of nuts other than peanuts are acceptable. Peanuts are part of the legume family and are therefore not included in a Paleo diet.
- **Tubers** – these include Jerusalem artichokes, cassava and taro, along with popular Paleo choices, yams and sweet potatoes.

Chapter Four: Non Paleo Foods

"If it comes in a box, you shouldn't be eating it" – Paleo saying

Essentially, any food that is processed is off the menu on a Paleo diet, including sugar-laden sodas and alcohol. Even "sugar-free" sodas are often full of harmful chemicals and so-called "healthy" juices can contain many hidden ingredients that are not so healthy. The main foods to avoid on a Paleo diet include the following:

- **Processed foods** – the more processes a food has been through, the lower the nutritional value is likely to be. Our "caveman" ancestors ate foods in their natural state but as a general rule in today's world of convenience foods, if a packaged product contains more than five ingredients, leave it on the shelf: this is particularly important if you are unable to pronounce the listed ingredients!

- **Cereal grains** – obvious examples of foods containing cereal grains are breakfast cereals and bread products but grains can be a hidden ingredient in a huge variety of processed foods. Avoiding grains also means avoiding meat sources from grain-fed animals.
- **Refined sugar** – cutting processed foods from your diet will also cut out refined sugars, as will cutting out obvious sugary foods such as pastries, cakes and candies.
- **Legumes** – this food group includes beans, soybeans, lentils and peas, also known as pulses in their dried form, and peanuts.
- **Refined vegetable oils** – only natural oils should be used for cooking but processed oils such as olive oil or canola oil can be used sparingly.
- **Salt** – once again, cutting processed foods from your diet will also cut out salt as it is a hidden ingredient in the majority of "convenience" foods. Salt should not be added to Paleo foods during cooking or before eating.

Foods to Restrict

If going without alcohol proves to be too restrictive, enjoying an occasional glass of red wine or tequila mixed with natural juice is considered acceptable on most Paleo-style diet plans. Fruit juices on their own should also be limited to an occasional "treat" only as they are high in sugar, and other beverages that can be enjoyed in moderation include coffee, tea, almond milk, coconut milk and coconut water. However, strict Paleo diet followers will avoid caffeine, alcohol, refined sugar and hidden ingredients completely by choosing to drink only water and herbal teas, and only occasionally making their own juices or nut milk at home when required.

Other restricted foods include:

- **Dairy** – not all Paleo advocates include dairy in their diet, but for those who do the general rule is to stay as close to a food's natural state as possible, so full fat milk or cheese for example.

- **Potatoes** – strict Paleo followers will avoid all potatoes as they are a "modern" food, but organically grown varieties are considered acceptable in moderation by many as they support the principle of adapting a Paleolithic diet to modern life.
- **Rice and Quinoa** – as with potatoes, these modern-day foods are acceptable in moderation on many Paleo-style diet plans.
- **Natural sugars** – all sugars, natural or refined, elevate insulin levels in your body and upset the energy balance. The naturally high sugar content of most fruits makes them a less beneficial source of carbohydrates in a Paleo diet than vegetables and for this reason should be eaten in moderation.

Paleo made simple key point # 2:

If it can be hunted, fished, or gathered, it's probably Paleo!

Chapter Five: Getting Started

"In order to live off a garden, you practically have to live in it" – Frank McKinney Hubbard

*#1st#*In an ideal world, growing your own organic produce at home would be the perfect way to ensure you always had a plentiful supply of fresh Paleo foods, but this is obviously not an approach that's going to work for everyone. The next best thing is to buy fresh and in season produce from your local farmers market but if you don't have access to markets in your area, it's perfectly possible to find the foods you need in your local grocery stores or online. Depending on where you live, you may find that many of your local stores have a good range of organic meats and produce to choose from but buying locally produced foodstuffs whenever possible is an important element of a Paleo lifestyle.

Paleo Store Cupboard Supplies

Fresh, natural foods are full of flavor on their own but some handy store cupboard cooking ingredients can help to add interest and variety to your Paleo meals. The best flavor combinations for you are down to personal taste but some basic cupboard supplies to get you started might include the following:

- **Canned goods** – this might include canned tomatoes or canned coconut milk for example, but ensure that any canned goods in your cupboards contain less than five ingredients ... and recognizable ingredients!
- **Mustard** – Dijon style or brown mustards are best but always check the listed ingredients, even if it says "organic" on the label.

- **Stock (or broth)** – making your own stock at home with meat bones or vegetables and then freezing it is an easy way to make sure you have a flavorsome, organic, low sodium and sugar free base for soups or casseroles whenever you need it. But, when buying back-up supplies for your store cupboard, look for organic brands that have the lowest sodium and sugar contents in the ingredients list.
- **Unrefined sea salt** – salt should only ever be added sparingly during cooking but when a recipe calls for salt, unrefined sea salt is the only Paleo choice.
- **Vinegar** – balsamic varieties or apple cider vinegar generally make the best choices, but check the ingredients list! Freshly squeezed lemon or lime juice make good alternatives in most recipes or dressings.
- **Fish sauce** – this provides a Paleo alternative to traditional soy sauce. Another soy sauce alternative is **coconut aminos**, and both can be used for marinating meat, dressing salads, or simply as seasoning.
- **Coconut or almond milk** – this is popularly used as a coffee or tea creamer but it also adds a delicious creaminess to smoothies, soups, or sauces.
- **Gluten-free flour** – popular choices are coconut or almond flour, both of which are easy to make at home. Store bought varieties vary in terms of the coarseness of the grind but gluten-free flour is a store cupboard essential for all types of Paleo baked goods. It's also useful as a thickener for gravies or sauces and can be used to help bind ingredients together in recipes such as crab cakes or meatballs.
- **Dehydrated coconut** – this can be used to give savory dishes a flavorful twist and it also provides a nutrient-packed addition to snacks and trail mixes.

Paleo Fresh Food Supplies

In general, fresh produce has a higher nutritional value than frozen or canned versions of the same but it's worth noting that some frozen food brands freeze the produce at source, actually helping it to retain a higher nutrient content than produce that may spend a little longer than ideal on the "fresh produce" shelf in a grocery store. Organic produce represents the healthiest and most natural choice as limited or no chemicals will have been used in the farming process, but *locally sourced* organic produce is always the very best choice. Packaging labels don't always tell the whole story but your local butcher or stall holder at your local farmers market can tell you everything you need to know!

Paleo made simple key point # 3:

Know what's in the food you eat and know how it was produced.

Chapter Six: Get Cooking!

"The greatest dishes are very simple" – Auguste Escoffier

There's possibly no better way to enjoy Paleo vegetables than in their raw, natural state with a delicious dressing and perhaps garnished with some nutritious nuts. However, Paleo foods can be cooked simply and quickly using any conventional method, with the only special consideration being your choice of cooking oil.

As a general rule, the preferred Paleo cooking oils are in fact the natural sources of saturated fat such as animal fats that are not liquid but solid at room temperature. These fats are more stable under high heat, meaning they will not transform into potentially hazardous free radicals through oxidization during cooking. Processed cooking oils such as peanut oil, soybean oil and corn oil are high in polyunsaturated fats and omega-6 fatty acids, and are therefore much more unstable when subjected to heat.

Paleo cooking Fats and Oils

- **Lard** – sourced from pigs, lard can be used for high heat cooking such as frying eggs, sautéing vegetables, stir-frying seafood, or grilling steaks. Leaf lard has a less "porky" flavor than other types available. When cooking, leftover lard can be poured into containers while it's hot and then stored in the refrigerator for re-use.
- **Animal fats (tallow)** – popular options include duck fat, goose fat and chicken fat. Tallow is rendered beef fat and is a good choice for deep-frying as it's very stable at high heats. It's also delicious when used for browning meats to make a stew or a curry.

- **Butter** – not all Paleo diets include dairy products but butter from grass-fed sources is generally acceptable for cooking purposes.
- **Ghee** – this is clarified butter and therefore suitable for non-dairy eaters. It's a popular choice in Indian cooking and it's very stable at high heats.
- **Coconut oil** – this is the staple cooking oil for many Paleo dieters as it's extremely versatile and contains over 90 percent saturated fat.
- **Palm oil** – this is another popular and versatile Paleo cooking choice but consideration must be given to the source as its production is now detrimental to the environment in areas of the world where rain forests are being cleared to make way for palm fruit production.
- **Olive oil** – with a high monounsaturated fat content, olive oil is unstable under heat but it's perfect for dressings on raw or cooked foods.

Other less stable Paleo oils that are best used for cooking at lower temperatures or for raw foods include the following:

- **Flaxseed oil** – also known as linseed oil.
- **Nut oils** – including hazelnut, pistachio and sesame seed oils.
- **Fish oil** – high in omega-3 fatty acids, but can give a slightly overpowering flavor!
- **Cod liver oil** – this is a popular choice in salad dressings combined with balsamic vinegar and crushed herbs, or in salsa combined with tomatoes, lime juice, peppers and chilies.

Paleo made simple key point # 4:

As a general rule, use saturated fats for cooking and monounsaturated oils for dressings.

Chapter Seven: Get Eating!

"Never eat more than you can lift" – Miss Piggy

The Paleo diet is essentially an "all-you-can-eat" diet of healthful, natural foods. When served up on a plate, a typical Paleo meal consists of unlimited vegetables – the more color and variety you have on your plate the better – a meat portion that's around the size of the palm of your hand, and an appropriate amount of fat for cooking or for garnishing.

Eating "all you want" sounds too good to be true but Paleo foods are so satisfying that overeating is never an issue. When you eat foods that are high in protein and natural fat, you feel satisfied at the end of every meal and you *stay* satisfied for much longer between meals compared to when eating a conventional diet of higher carb foods. There's certainly no calorie counting when aiming to lose weight on a Paleo diet, and there's no "starvation" required as you simply eat whenever you're hungry!

Classic Paleo Meals

Switching from a conventional diet to a Paleo diet often means changing the way you think about food, and the foods you "traditionally" eat at certain times of day in particular. For example, in many parts of the world a traditional breakfast consists of a bowl of cereal with milk followed by a slice of toast with a sugary spread, and a traditional lunch might be a sandwich on the go or a pasta dish with crusty bread on the side. Going Paleo means breaking those habitual eating patterns and embracing a new approach to fuelling your body.

Typical Paleo breakfast foods:

Starting your day with meat on your plate rather than toast may seem strange at first but those who make the switch report feeling physically and mentally ready for the day ahead and no longer trapped in a cycle of bouncing from one sugary snack to another to keep them going until lunch. The following breakfast suggestions are only the very tip of the iceberg in terms of popular Paleo choices.

- **Eggs** – fried in bacon fat or made into a nutritious omelet with herbs of your choice.
- **Bacon** – served with eggs or in an omelet.
- **Pancakes** – made with almond flour and served with fruit.
- **Fruit salad** – made with berries when in season.
- **Fruit smoothie** – made with coconut milk and fruits of your choice or add vegetables to kick start your day with a nutrient-packed green smoothie.

Typical Paleo lunch foods:

Once again, the following suggestions are simply a few ideas to get your mouth watering! The possibilities are virtually endless and limited only by your time restraints at lunchtime.

- **Soup** – how about Thai chicken soup, vegetable gazpacho, or bacon and parsnip soup to name just a few?
- **Frittata** – made with sweet potato and ingredients of your choice; how about zucchini, onion, or bacon and spinach to name just a few?
- **Salad** – with everything from a crisp Waldorf salad to a duck and pomegranate salad, there are hundreds of nutritious Paleo salad combinations. Hot salads with chicken or bacon are also delicious alternatives.

Typical Paleo evening meal foods:

The variety of meals that can be made quickly and easily using only Paleo foods is enormous, and you don't need to be a gourmet chef to cook up delicious meals that suit every taste when you are using naturally flavorsome, fresh and organic produce. Here a just a few examples:

- **Stir fries** – how about spicy shrimp, chili beef, tomato and egg, or chicken and pesto to name just a few?
- **Fish dishes** – for example; baked salmon, grilled trout, crab cakes, or sardines wrapped in bacon.
- **Curried dishes** – for example; chicken, shrimp, beef, or cauliflower with bacon and cashew nut curry.
- **Stews** – beef, pork and chicken all make hearty stews, and how about a seafood stew, or lamb or venison?
- **Meat dishes** – everything from shepherd's pie made with sweet potatoes through steak and eggs to roast duck or chicken. There are literally hundreds of options!
- **Side dishes** – vegetables fill the biggest portion of your Paleo plate but vegetable dishes need never be boring; how about roasted beets with walnut vinaigrette, spicy cauliflower, or Brussels sprouts with bacon?

And Paleo Desserts!

Paleo dieters with a sweet tooth can also enjoy a variety of treats and desserts, including these tempting suggestions:

- **Cookies and cakes** – made with coconut or almond flour.
- **Pumpkin pie**
- **Banana bread**
- **Coconut ice cream**

Paleo made simple key point # 5:

Stick to simple fresh food combinations and build your "recipe book" around the flavorsome natural tastes you discover.

Chapter Eight: Paleo Diet for Fat Loss

"Don't dig your grave with your own knife and fork" – English Proverb

In simple terms, our bodies store fat so that we can use it for energy when we need it. In the days of our "caveman" ancestors, having adequate fat reserves was a matter of basic survival, keeping us alive when food was scarce. Of course, in today's world, it's rare that food is ever scarce and the general trend in the Western world is that we eat too much rather than too little. Excess calories consumed on a daily basis are converted to fat and stored by our bodies for future use, but, because food is never in short supply, our fat supplies are never used ... and so we become fat!

Losing weight is essentially a matter of calories in versus calories out, or getting the balance right between the amount of food you eat and the amount of energy you burn doing everyday activities. However, losing weight and losing fat are not necessarily one and the same. To lose unwanted and unhealthy levels of body fat, your body must learn how to burn fat for fuel on a daily basis, and this means exercising in a way that boosts your metabolism and promotes the release of fat burning hormones. One of the most effective ways to promote fat burning is known as interval training.

Interval Training

Interval training is simply alternating short periods of high intensity effort with periods of lower intensity effort across the total duration of your workout. For example, a runner might incorporate interval training into their session by alternating short bursts of fast-paced running with slightly longer periods of steady-paced running for the duration of their run. The same can be applied to walking, with frequent short bursts of faster paced efforts incorporated into a regular walk route. The efforts don't need to be precise or timed in any way, with many exercisers choosing to use natural landmarks such as trees or park benches to mark a change of pace.

Interval training is known as fartlek training in Sweden, its place of origin. Fartlek translates as "speed play".

In a nutshell, continuously varying the intensity of your workout makes your body work harder, making it a time-efficient as well as effective way to maximize the benefits of exercise.

The key to boosting your metabolism, and therefore increasing your ability to burn fat, is to increase the amount of lean muscle mass you have. The more lean muscle you have, the more calories you burn every hour of every day – even when you are asleep. However, increasing your muscle mass does not mean "bulking up" like Mr. or Mrs. Universe! Lean muscle provides functional strength and gives your body a naturally sculpted physique that oozes health and vitality. It's not even necessary to work out with weights to promote lean muscle growth, and simple bodyweight exercises that can be performed at home are all you need to stimulate the release of fat burning hormones.

The following exercise routines require minimal or no equipment and each session targets only the major muscle groups in order to maximize the benefits in the minimal time.

Beginner Level Exercise Routine

Your body adapts to repetitive new pressures placed upon it, meaning that if you are a newcomer to exercise, exercises that feel challenging in the beginning will very quickly become much less challenging through regular repetition. However, in order to adapt, your body needs time to recover, and for this reason you should allow at least one rest day between sessions. For example, the following program could be scheduled for Monday, Wednesday and Friday each week with one day of active recovery included over the weekend. Active recovery is simply taking part in a gentle form of exercise such as a leisurely walk and it is particularly useful if you experience tightness in your muscles after exercise.

Important note: always check with your medical professional before starting any new program of exercise.

Monday (or day of your choice)

Warm up your body ready for exercise by simply moving around! This might take the form of marching around your home or simply marching on the spot. Include some arm circling in a backstroke swimming action to warm up your upper body joints.

Squats – this exercise targets all of the major muscles in your legs, including your butt.

- Stand with your feet placed at slightly wider than hip-width apart. Allow your toes to angle out slightly so that your knees will follow the line of your toes as you bend your legs to squat down.

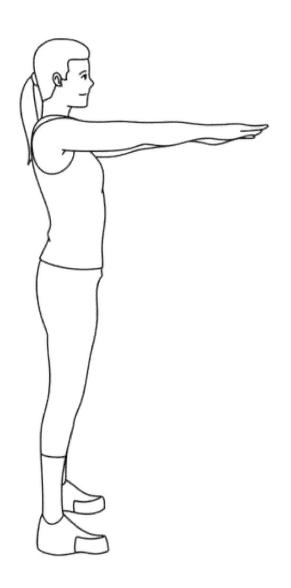

- Bend your knees to squat down, as if about to sit back into an imaginary chair, aiming to lower your butt to the level of your knees – or lower if it feels comfortable to do so.
- Raise your arms in front of your body to shoulder height as you squat down, although you may find it helpful initially to place one hand against a wall or solid object as a balance aid.
- Reverse the movements to return to the starting stance and then repeat the exercise for a total of 12 to 15 squats.
- Breathe normally throughout and stay in control of the movements at every stage.

Standing Push-Ups – this exercise targets your chest and triceps, the muscles which form the back of your upper arm.

- Stand facing a wall and place yourself around arm's-length away from it.
- Position your hands on the wall at shoulder-height and slightly wider than shoulder-width apart.

- Bend your elbows to lean in toward the wall, keeping good posture throughout your body as you do so. Allow your heels to lift up from the floor as you lean in.
- Push back from the wall to return to the starting stance before repeating the exercise to complete 12 to 15 standing push-ups.
- It's important to maintain correct posture in your back and this can be aided by imagining you are trying to pull your tummy in toward your spine. However, avoid holding your breath by focusing on breathing in as you lean in and breathing out as you push back each time.

Seated Row – this exercise targets the muscles of your upper back and biceps, the muscles which form the front of your upper arm.

You will need a stretchy exercise band or resistance band for this exercise; these are readily available in most sports stores or online and are relatively inexpensive.

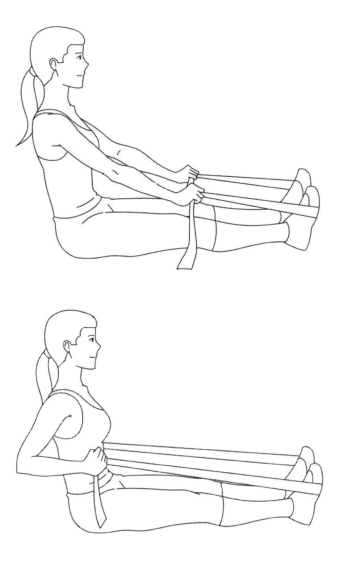

o   Sit on the floor with your legs stretched out in front of you.

- o Place the exercise band around the bottom of your feet to create a "rowing machine" effect with one handle in each hand.
- o Move your arms to take your elbows behind the line of your body in a "rowing" action, maintaining an upright posture in your upper body throughout.
- o Staying in control of the band, allow your arms to return to the starting position, before repeating the movements to complete 12 to 15 seated rows.
- o Breathe normally throughout and experiment with different resistances by shortening or lengthening the band to find the correct degree of challenge for you.

Wednesday (or at least 48 hours after your last session)

This session is a cardio session designed to raise your heart rate and breathing rate. Warm up your body as above.

Squat and Jump

- Perform the squat exercise as detailed above but with your hands placed by your ears rather than held out in front.

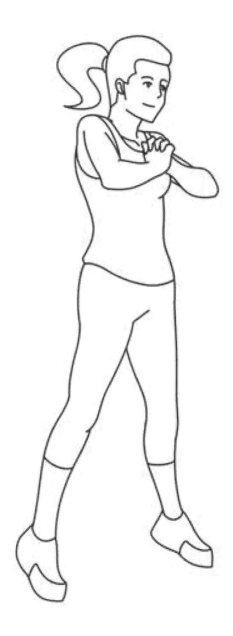

- At the end of the squat movement, spring up into the starting position to finish with an energized bounce from the floor!

- Repeat the sequence of moves to complete 12 to 15 "squat jumps" in total.
- Aim to stay light on your toes as you spring up and land, allowing your hip, knee and ankle joints to remain relaxed as natural shock absorbers.

Jumping Jacks

- Stand with your feet together and your arms by your sides.
- Jump both feet out to the side, raising your arms out to the side and above your head simultaneously.

- Jump your feet and arms back to the starting stance, before repeating the movements to complete 12 to 15 jumping jacks in total.
- A lower impact version of this exercise is to move only one foot and arm at a time, alternating from side to side in a "half jack" movement i.e. right foot and right arm out and back followed by left foot and left arm out and back.

Squat and Punch – this exercise combines the squat movement to work your legs with punching movements to work your arms ... a combo that's guaranteed to raise your heart rate!

- As you squat, punch alternate arms out in front of you as quickly as you comfortably can.

- Aim to continue the "rapid fire" squat and punch movements for 30 seconds, gradually building up to 60 seconds as your fitness improves.

Friday (or at least 48 hours after your last session)

This session should be a repeat of Monday's routine:

Squats – 12 to 15 repetitions

Standing Push-Ups – 12 to 15 repetitions

Seated Row – 12 to 15 repetitions

Intermediate Level Exercise Routine

As your fitness improves, the beginner level exercise routine can be advanced as follows:

Monday (or day of your choice)

Front Lunges – this exercise targets the major muscles in your legs.

- Warm up by jogging, walking, or marching in place for several minutes.
- Stand with your feet placed at hip-width apart, placing one hand against a wall or solid object to aid your balance if necessary.
- Step forward with your right foot, then bend both legs to lower your left knee toward the floor, allowing your left heel to lift from the floor as you lunge.
- Maintain an upright posture throughout the exercise, avoiding any tilting in your upper body.

- Return to the starting stance, before switching legs to repeat the exercise with your left leg stepping forward.
- Continue to alternate legs, aiming to complete 10 to 12 repetitions on each leg.

Incline Push-Ups – this exercise adds intensity to the standing push-ups exercise detailed above. The major muscle groups worked are the chest and triceps.

- Stand facing a kitchen counter, solid table, park bench, or any solid object that's of a suitable height. The greater the incline, the more intense the exercise becomes.

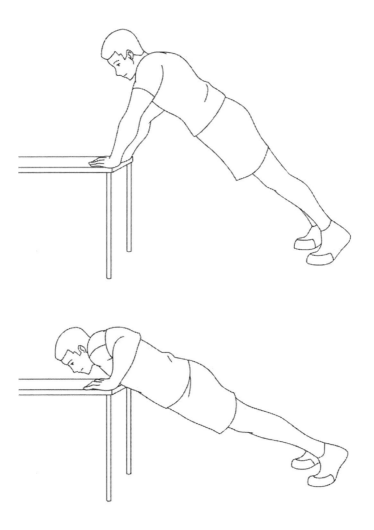

- Place your hands at slightly wider than shoulder-width apart and maintain good posture throughout your body as you move into the incline starting position.
- Bend your elbows to lower your chest toward the counter and then reverse the movements to return to the starting stance.
- Breathe in as you lower your body and breathe out as you push it up again.
- Aim to complete 12 to 15 repetitions.

Squat and Row – this exercise requires an exercise band. The leg muscles are targeted along with the upper back and biceps.

- Place your feet on the exercise band and cross it over in front of your legs, holding the handles with straight arms as shown below.

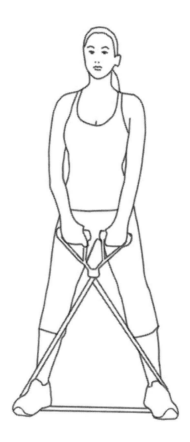

- Squat down so that the band is relaxed, before standing up and raising your hands up under your chin with your elbows leading the way.

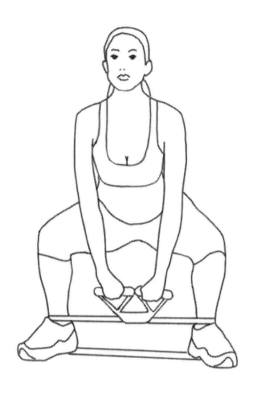

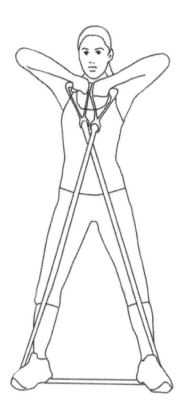

- Repeat the sequence to complete 12 to 15 squat and row movements in total.
- Breathe normally throughout and stay in control of the resistance at every stage.

Wednesday (or at least 48 hours after your last session)

This cardio session is designed to raise your breathing and heart rate, and get you sweating!

Step-Ups

- Stand facing a low step such as the bottom stair in your home.

- Step onto the step with your right foot leading followed by your left foot, and then step back down with right foot leading followed by left foot.

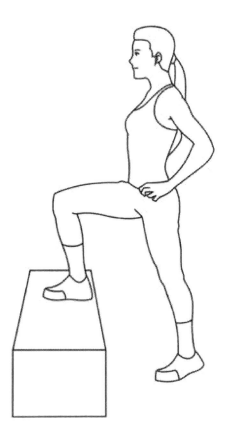

- Now set yourself the challenge of completing as many step-ups as possible within 30 seconds, then switch legs to complete another 30 seconds with your left leg leading the way.

Push-Ups

- Set yourself the target of completing as many push-ups as possible within 60 seconds. Begin with the incline push-up version and switch to the standing push-up version (beginner level exercise routine) if necessary in order to complete the full minute without stopping.

Squat and Row

* Set yourself the target of completing as many exercise band squat and row exercises as possible within 60 seconds. Faster movements increase the intensity of the exercise but it's important to stay in control of the movements at every stage.

Mini Circuit

Create a cardio challenge by tagging all three exercises together to create a mini circuit. The aim is to complete three circuits of three full minutes of non-stop exercise, three times around ... with only 60 seconds of rest between each circuit!

* **Step-ups x 60 seconds / push-ups x 60 seconds / squat and row x 60 seconds**
* Allow yourself a 60 second rest then repeat.
* **Step-ups x 60 seconds / push-ups x 60 seconds / squat and row x 60 seconds**
* Allow yourself a 60 second rest and then repeat for the third and final time.
* **Step-ups x 60 seconds / push-ups x 60 seconds / squat and row x 60 seconds**

Friday (or at least 48 hours after your last session)

This session should be a repeat of Monday's session:

Front Lunges – 10 to 12 repetitions on each leg

Incline Push-Ups – 12 to 15 repetitions

Squat and Row – 12 to 15 repetitions

Paleo made easy key point # 6:

Keep it simple, keep it fun, and keep it up!

In terms of fitness training, it's a common misconception that more is better. However, in terms of fat loss, less is definitely more. A regular exercise program of three or four days per week and sessions of no more than 30 minutes each time is much more effective than working your body to the point of exhaustion every day of the week. Allow your body to adapt to the new demands by taking regular rest days between training days, getting quality sleep every day, and fuelling your activities with quality food and plentiful water.

The bottom line is that a Paleo lifestyle is all about keeping things simple: so simple that even a "caveman" could do it! Modern life and modern choices can make our lives overcomplicated, so it's time to learn from the simple wisdom of our ancient ancestors – eat well, sleep well, stay active and live well.

74 Satisfying Recipes to Regain Your Potential

PALEO BREAKFAST

1. Maple Coconut Pancakes
Servings: 4
Preparation time: 10 minutes
Cook time: 16 minutes
Ready in: 26 minutes

```
Nutrition Facts
Serving Size 208 g

Amount Per Serving
Calories 399          Calories from Fat 223
                              % Daily Value*
Total Fat 24.7g                        38%
   Saturated Fat 14.5g                 73%
   Trans Fat 0.0g
Cholesterol 164mg                      55%
Sodium 623mg                           26%
Total Carbohydrates 38.3g              13%
   Dietary Fiber 3.7g                  15%
   Sugars 30.1g
Protein 9.7g

Vitamin A 5%          •      Vitamin C 9%
Calcium 9%            •          Iron 16%

Nutrition Grade C-
* Based on a 2000 calorie diet
```

Ingredients
- 4 pasture-fed, free-range eggs
- 1 cup pure coconut milk
- 1/2 cup pure maple syrup
- 2 teaspoons pure vanilla extract
- 1/2 cup coconut flour

- 1 teaspoon baking soda
- 1/2 cup almonds, chopped
- 1/4 teaspoon ground cinnamon
- 1/2 teaspoon unrefined sea salt
- coconut oil for greasing
- 1 cup blueberries

Directions

- **Beat** together the eggs, coconut milk, 1 tablespoon maple syrup, and vanilla in a large bowl.
- **Whisk** together the coconut flour, baking soda, chopped almonds, cinnamon, and salt in another bowl. Add the flour mixture to the egg mixture and beat for about 1 minute to combine. Let the batter sit for about 2 minutes.
- **Grease** a medium pan with coconut oil then place pan over medium-low heat.
- **Pour** batter onto pan, about 3 tablespoons for each pancake. Brown for about 2-3 minutes each side.
- **Serve** warm and top each pancake with 1 tablespoon maple syrup and blueberries.

2. Scrambled Eggs and Mushrooms

Servings: 2
Preparation time: 10 minutes
Cook time: 8 minutes
Ready in: 18 minutes

Nutrition Facts

Serving Size 155 g

Amount Per Serving

Calories 273	Calories from Fat 218

	% Daily Value*
Total Fat 24.2g	**37%**
Saturated Fat 6.1g	**31%**
Trans Fat 0.0g	
Cholesterol 280mg	**93%**
Sodium 153mg	**6%**
Total Carbohydrates 3.9g	**1%**
Dietary Fiber 0.7g	**3%**
Sugars 2.2g	
Protein 11.6g	

Vitamin A 17%	•	Vitamin C 25%
Calcium 13%	•	Iron 10%

Nutrition Grade B-
* Based on a 2000 calorie diet

Ingredients
- 2 cloves garlic, minced
- 3 tablespoon extra-virgin olive oil
- 1/4 cup onions, chopped
- 1/4 cup fresh mushrooms, sliced
- 1/4 cup green bell peppers, chopped
- 5 pasture-fed, free-range eggs
- 1/4 cup pure coconut milk
- 1/4 cup fresh tomato, chopped
- 1/4 cup grass-fed raw milk Cheddar cheese, shredded (recommended: Organic Pastures or PastureLand True Raw Milk Cheddar)
- 1/2 cup fresh cilantro leaves, chopped
  Note: For strict Paleo version, omit cheese

Directions
- **Heat** olive oil in a skillet over medium-high heat. Sauté garlic in oil until lightly browned.

59

- **Stir** in onions, mushrooms, and green bell peppers, cook until onions are soft and translucent.
- **Beat** eggs in a medium bowl then add the coconut milk. Add egg mixture, tomatoes, and cheese to the mushroom mixture; cook for about 1 minute, or until eggs are set.
- **Serve** topped with chopped cilantro.

3. Herbed Golden Scotch Eggs

Servings: 6
Preparation time: 10 minutes
Cook time: 20 minutes
Ready in: 30 minutes

Nutrition Facts

Serving Size 198 g

Amount Per Serving

Calories 364   Calories from Fat 258

	% Daily Value*
Total Fat 28.7g	**44%**
Saturated Fat 19.9g	**99%**
Trans Fat 0.0g	
Cholesterol 42mg	**14%**
Sodium 109mg	**5%**
Total Carbohydrates 6.6g	**2%**
Dietary Fiber 4.0g	**16%**
Sugars 0.9g	
Protein 18.7g	

Vitamin A 27%	•	Vitamin C 34%
Calcium 5%	•	Iron 10%

Nutrition Grade C+
* Based on a 2000 calorie diet

Ingredients
- 6 pasture-fed, free-range eggs
- 1/2 pound organic pork mince
- 1/2 teaspoon Dijon mustard
- 3/4 tablespoon marjoram, chopped
- 1/2 teaspoon unrefined sea salt
- 1/4 teaspoon ground black pepper
- 1 1/2 cups parsley, chopped
- 2 onion chives, chopped
- 1/2 cup coconut flour
- 1 egg, beaten

- Coconut oil for deep frying

Directions
- **Preheat** oven to 350 degrees f.
- **Boil** eggs in a pot of water, about 4 minutes. Let cool, peel, and set aside.
- **Combine** pork mince, mustard, marjoram, salt, pepper, parsley, and chives. Flatten meat mixture and mold evenly onto each egg.
- **Dip** each meat-coated egg in the egg batter then coat with the coconut flour.
- **Heat** coconut oil in a pan over medium heat. Deep fry scotch eggs in coconut oil until golden brown then place on a baking sheet.
- **Bake** for 10 to 12 minutes. Cut the eggs in half and serve.

4. Summer Fresh Fruit Salad

Servings: 7
Preparation time: 15 minutes
Cook time: 10 minutes
Ready in: 25 minutes

Nutrition Facts

Serving Size 249 g

Amount Per Serving

Calories 299	Calories from Fat 126
	% Daily Value*
Total Fat 14.0g	**22%**
Saturated Fat 1.2g	**6%**
Trans Fat 0.0g	
Cholesterol 0mg	**0%**
Sodium 8mg	**0%**
Total Carbohydrates 41.4g	**14%**
Dietary Fiber 8.4g	**33%**
Sugars 26.3g	
Protein 7.7g	

Vitamin A 20%	•	Vitamin C 107%
Calcium 11%	•	Iron 9%

Nutrition Grade A
* Based on a 2000 calorie diet

Ingredients
- 1/3 cup fresh lemon juice

- 2/3 cup fresh orange juice
- 2 tablespoons raw honey
- 1/2 teaspoon grated orange zest
- 1/2 teaspoon grated lemon zest
- 1 teaspoon pure vanilla extract
- 1 teaspoon ground cinnamon
- 1 cup cubed pears
- 2 cups strawberries, hulled and sliced
- 1 cup cantaloupe balls
- 3 bananas, sliced
- 2 oranges, peeled and sectioned
- 1 cup seedless grapes
- 2 cups almonds, sliced

Directions

- **Combine** orange juice and zest, lemon juice and zest, and honey in a saucepan over medium-high heat and bring to a boil.
- **Reduce** heat to medium-low, then simmer mixture for 5 minutes, or until syrupy. Remove pan from heat, and stir in vanilla and cinnamon. Cool and set aside.
- **Place** the fruits in a large bowl and toss with the prepared sauce.
- **Cover** and chill before serving.

5. Fresh Fruit 'n Spinach Smoothie

Servings: 2
Ready in: 8 minutes

Nutrition Facts

Serving Size 229 g

Amount Per Serving

Calories 275   Calories from Fat 124

	% Daily Value*
Total Fat 13.7g	**21%**
Saturated Fat 8.9g	**44%**
Trans Fat 0.0g	
Cholesterol 2mg	**1%**
Sodium 51mg	**2%**
Total Carbohydrates 31.5g	**11%**
Dietary Fiber 9.6g	**38%**
Sugars 23.0g	
Protein 8.0g	

Vitamin A 1%	•	Vitamin C 34%
Calcium 12%	•	Iron 10%

Nutrition Grade B

* Based on a 2000 calorie diet

Ingredients
- 1/2 cup pure coconut milk
- 3/4 cup almond cream
- 1 fresh cold banana, peeled and chopped
- 1/4 cup flax seed
- 1 teaspoon raw honey
- 1/2 cup frozen strawberries
- 1/2 cup frozen raspberries
- 1 cup spinach leaves

Directions
- **Place** all ingredients in a blender and blend until smooth.
- **Chill**, pour into glasses, and serve.

6. Honey Glazed Pumpkin Donuts

Servings: 4
Preparation time: 15 minutes
Cook time: 18-20 minutes

Ready in: 33 minutes

Nutrition Facts

Serving Size 117 g

Amount Per Serving	
Calories 304	Calories from Fat 184
	% Daily Value*
Total Fat 20.4g	**31%**
Saturated Fat 15.6g	**78%**
Trans Fat 0.0g	
Cholesterol 82mg	**27%**
Sodium 344mg	**14%**
Total Carbohydrates 25.4g	**8%**
Dietary Fiber 7.4g	**29%**
Sugars 13.4g	
Protein 5.8g	

Vitamin A 66%	•	Vitamin C 4%
Calcium 6%	•	Iron 10%

Nutrition Grade D+

* Based on a 2000 calorie diet

Ingredients

- 1/2 cup coconut flour
- 1/2 teaspoon baking soda
- 1 tablespoon pumpkin pie spice
- 1/4 teaspoon unrefined sea salt
- 2 pasture-fed, free-range eggs
- 1/2 cup pure light coconut milk
- 1/3 cup pumpkin puree
- 3 tablespoon pure maple syrup
- 2 tablespoon coconut oil + 1 tablespoon for greasing

Honey Glaze:

- 2 teaspoons coconut oil, softened
- 1 teaspoon raw honey, softened
- 1 tablespoon ground cinnamon
- 1/2 teaspoon pure vanilla extract

Directions

- **Preheat** oven to 350 degrees f. Grease a donut mold with 1 tablespoon coconut oil.
- **Mix** together the coconut flour, baking soda, pumpkin pie spice, and salt in a large bowl. In another bowl, whisk together the eggs, coconut milk, pumpkin, maple syrup, and coconut oil.

- **Add** wet mixture to the dry mixture. Add a tablespoon of coconut milk if the batter is dry. Pour the batter into the donut mold.
- **Bake** for 18 to 20 minutes, until donuts are golden brown or toothpick inserted in the center of donut comes out clean or with only a few crumbs sticking to it.
- **Cool** donuts for 5 minutes in the pan then place in a wire rack.
- **Stir** together all the ingredients for the glaze in a medium bowl. Set the bowl over hot water for 30 seconds; whisk mixture until creamy. Spread the glaze over the top of donuts using a butter knife.

7. Roasted Bacon-Wrapped Asparagus over Brown Rice

Servings: 4
Preparation time: 15 minutes
Cook time: 1 hour and 15 minutes
Ready in: 1 hour and 30 minutes

Nutrition Facts

Serving Size 308 g

Amount Per Serving

Calories 322	Calories from Fat 114

	% Daily Value*
Total Fat 12.7g	**20%**
Saturated Fat 5.8g	**29%**
Trans Fat 0.0g	
Cholesterol 16mg	**5%**
Sodium 354mg	**15%**
Total Carbohydrates 42.5g	**14%**
Dietary Fiber 4.2g	**17%**
Sugars 2.9g	
Protein 10.6g	

Vitamin A 21%	•	Vitamin C 12%
Calcium 5%	•	Iron 19%

Nutrition Grade B
* Based on a 2000 calorie diet

Ingredients
- 1 pound asparagus, ends trimmed

- 2 tablespoons grass-fed raw milk butter (recommended: Organic Valley)
- 12 slices nitrite/nitrate-free bacon
- 1 tablespoon Dijon mustard
- 4 cloves garlic, chopped

Brown Rice:

- 1 cup long-grain gluten-free brown rice
- 2 cups water
- 1/2 teaspoon unrefined sea salt

Note: For strict Paleo version, go for Cauliflower Rice (see Recipe No. 55) instead of Brown Rice

Directions

- **Rinse** brown rice under cold water.
- **Boil** water in a medium saucepan over high heat. Add the rice and stir in the salt. Reduce the heat to low. Cover the saucepan and simmer for 45 to 50 minutes, or until the rice is tender. Remove pan from heat, cover and let sit to steam for 10 minutes more.
- **Preheat** oven to 425 degrees F. Line a baking sheet with aluminum foil.
- **Divide** asparagus into 12 bundles (about 3 pieces each).
- **Rub** each piece of asparagus with butter.
- **Combine** mustard and garlic in a small bowl.
- **Roll** a slice of bacon around each bundle of asparagus then sprinkle with the mustard mixture.
- **Roast** in preheated oven for 20-25 minutes, or until bacon is crispy. Serve over brown rice.

8. Nutty Porridge

Servings: 4
Preparation time: 8 hours and 10 minutes
Cook time: 5 minutes
Ready in: 8 hours and 15 minutes

Nutrition Facts

Serving Size 147 g

Amount Per Serving

Calories 386	Calories from Fat 220

	% Daily Value*
Total Fat 24.5g	**38%**
Saturated Fat 2.6g	**13%**
Trans Fat 0.0g	
Cholesterol 0mg	**0%**
Sodium 193mg	**8%**
Total Carbohydrates 38.2g	**13%**
Dietary Fiber 4.8g	**19%**
Sugars 21.7g	
Protein 10.3g	

Vitamin A 6%	•	Vitamin C 6%
Calcium 7%	•	Iron 14%

Nutrition Grade B+

* Based on a 2000 calorie diet

Ingredients
- 1/2 cup each raw almonds, cashews, and walnuts (soaked overnight in a lightly salted water)
- 1 ripe banana
- 2 cups organic low-fat almond milk
- 2 teaspoons raw honey
- 1 teaspoons ground cinnamon
- 1/4 teaspoon unrefined sea salt
- 1/2 cup raisins

Directions
- **Rinse** and drain nuts.
- **Place** all ingredients in a blender and blend until smooth.
- **Pour** mixture into a pot and simmer for 5 minutes over medium-high heat.
- **Stir** in raisins. Ladle porridge into bowls, cool for a few minutes, and serve.

9. Veggie Herb Omelet

Servings: 2
Preparation time: 10 minutes
Cook time: 12 minutes
Ready in: 22 minutes

Nutrition Facts

Serving Size 272 g

Amount Per Serving

Calories 314   Calories from Fat 222

	% Daily Value*
Total Fat 24.7g	**38%**
Saturated Fat 7.4g	**37%**
Trans Fat 0.0g	
Cholesterol 323mg	**108%**
Sodium 819mg	**34%**
Total Carbohydrates 14.0g	**5%**
Dietary Fiber 3.7g	**15%**
Sugars 6.7g	
Protein 11.1g	

Vitamin A 144%   •   Vitamin C 156%
Calcium 6%   •   Iron 14%

Nutrition Grade C
* Based on a 2000 calorie diet

Ingredients
- 2 tablespoons extra-virgin olive oil, divided
- 1 clove garlic, minced
- 1 small onion, chopped
- 1 green bell pepper, chopped
- 1/2 cup carrots, sliced
- 1/2 cup tomatoes, diced
- 4 pasture-fed, free-range eggs
- 3/4 teaspoon unrefined sea salt
- 1 dash ground black pepper
- 2 tablespoons pure coconut milk
- 1 tablespoon chives
- 1 tablespoon basil
- 1 tablespoon parsley

Directions
- **Heat** 1 tablespoon olive oil in a skillet over medium heat.

- **Sauté** garlic in olive oil until lightly browned. Stir in onion, bell pepper, carrots, and tomatoes, cook for 5 minutes, or until tender. Place cooked vegetables in a bowl then sprinkle with 1/4 teaspoon sea salt. Set aside.
- **Beat** together the eggs, 1/2 teaspoon salt, pepper, and coconut milk. Stir in chives, basil, and parsley.
- **Heat** the remaining 1 tablespoon olive oil in the same skillet over medium heat.
- **Add** the egg mixture and cook for 4 minutes, or until set.
- **Spoon** the vegetable mixture into the center of the omelet then fold one edge of the omelet over the vegetables. Cook for another 2 minutes. Place omelet in serving plates, slice in half, and serve.

10. Crispy Classic Waffles

Servings: 4
Preparation time: 10 minutes
Cook time: 25 minutes
Ready in: 35 minutes

Nutrition Facts

Serving Size 219 g

Amount Per Serving

Calories 282	Calories from Fat 134

	% Daily Value*
Total Fat 14.9g	**23%**
Saturated Fat 5.3g	**27%**
Trans Fat 0.0g	
Cholesterol 82mg	**27%**
Sodium 558mg	**23%**
Total Carbohydrates 33.8g	**11%**
Dietary Fiber 2.0g	**8%**
Sugars 26.0g	
Protein 5.9g	

Vitamin A 2%	•	Vitamin C 6%
Calcium 7%	•	Iron 8%

Nutrition Grade D-
* Based on a 2000 calorie diet

Ingredients
- 2 cups almond flour
- 1/2 teaspoon unrefined sea salt
- 1 teaspoon baking soda mixed with 2 tablespoons lemon juice

- 2 pasture-fed, free-range eggs
- 1 1/2 cups pure light coconut milk
- 1/4 cup applesauce
- 2 tablespoons raw honey
- 1 teaspoon pure vanilla extract
- 1 teaspoon ground cinnamon
- 5 tablespoons pure maple syrup

Directions
- **Preheat** waffle iron to desired temperature.
- **Mix** together the flour, baking soda mixture, and salt in a large bowl.
- **Beat** together the eggs, coconut milk, applesauce, honey, vanilla, and cinnamon in a separate bowl then pour into the flour mixture. Mix batter until well blended.
- **Ladle** the batter into the waffle iron and cook until crisp.
- **Top** each waffle with 1 tablespoon maple syrup.

11. Smoked Salmon Frittata

Servings: 4
Preparation time: 10 minutes
Cook time: 30 minutes
Ready in: 1 hour

Nutrition Facts

Serving Size 242 g

Amount Per Serving	
Calories 362	Calories from Fat 265

	% Daily Value*
Total Fat 29.4g	**45%**
Saturated Fat 7.0g	**35%**
Trans Fat 0.1g	
Cholesterol 264mg	**88%**
Sodium 511mg	**21%**
Total Carbohydrates 10.5g	**3%**
Dietary Fiber 2.8g	**11%**
Sugars 5.8g	
Protein 16.1g	

Vitamin A 83%	Vitamin C 255%
Calcium 6%	Iron 12%

Nutrition Grade B-

* Based on a 2000 calorie diet

Ingredients
- 4 tablespoons olive oil
- 1/2 teaspoon of garlic
- 2 medium shallots, chopped
- 1/2 teaspoon unrefined sea salt
- 1/4 teaspoon ground black pepper
- 4 ounces pepper smoked salmon
- 4 red bell peppers, seeded and chopped
- 6 pasture-fed, free-range eggs
- 2 tablespoons pure coconut milk
- 1/4 teaspoon dried thyme
- 1/2 teaspoon dried rosemary
- 1 teaspoon fresh dill, chopped

Directions
- **Preheat** the oven to 350 degrees f (175 degrees c).

71

- **Heat** olive oil in a medium oven-safe skillet over medium heat.
- **Sauté** garlic in olive oil until lightly browned. Stir in shallots, and season with salt and pepper; cook, until shallots are translucent.
- **Add** the salmon and red bell pepper, cook for about 5 minutes; stirring often.
- **Whisk** together the eggs and coconut milk, stir in thyme, rosemary, and dill then pour mixture over the salmon in the skillet. Cook until the edges are firm.
- **Place** the skillet in oven, and bake for 20 minutes, until golden brown. Place frittata on a plate, cut into wedges, and serve.

12. Vanilla Berry Crepes

Servings: 4
Preparation time: 15 minutes
Cook time: 24 minutes
Ready in: 39 minutes

Nutrition Facts

Serving Size 321 g

Amount Per Serving

Calories 381   Calories from Fat 229

	% Daily Value*
Total Fat 25.5g	**39%**
Saturated Fat 14.2g	**71%**
Trans Fat 0.0g	
Cholesterol 197mg	**66%**
Sodium 318mg	**13%**
Total Carbohydrates 30.9g	**10%**
Dietary Fiber 4.0g	**16%**
Sugars 23.3g	
Protein 5.7g	

Vitamin A 8%	•	Vitamin C 90%
Calcium 22%	•	Iron 8%

Nutrition Grade D+
* Based on a 2000 calorie diet

Ingredients
- 3 pasture-fed, free-range egg yolks
- 2 tablespoons pure vanilla extract
- 1 1/2 cups pure coconut milk

- 2 tablespoons raw honey
- 1 1/2 cups gluten-free almond flour
- 1/3 cup grass-fed raw milk butter, melted (recommended: Organic Valley)
- 1/4 teaspoon ground cinnamon
- 1/4 teaspoon nutmeg
- 1/2 teaspoon unrefined sea salt
- Coconut oil for greasing
- 2 cups fresh strawberries, sliced
- 2 cups fresh blueberries

Directions
- **Whisk** together the egg yolks, vanilla, coconut milk, and honey in a large bowl.
- **Add** the flour, butter, cinnamon, nutmeg, and salt; whisk thoroughly.
- **Grease** a crepe pan with coconut oil then place pan over medium heat.
- **Pour** and spread about 1/4 cup of batter (for each crepe) into the pan. Brown crepes on both sides.
- **Fill** crepes with strawberries and blueberries to serve.

13. Choco Banana Muffins Recipe

Servings: 8
Preparation time: 10 minutes
Cook time: 15-20 minutes
Ready in: 25 minutes

Nutrition Facts

Serving Size 128 g

Amount Per Serving

Calories 393	Calories from Fat 220

	% Daily Value*
Total Fat 24.5g	**38%**
Saturated Fat 10.4g	**52%**
Trans Fat 0.0g	
Cholesterol 41mg	**14%**
Sodium 494mg	**21%**
Total Carbohydrates 41.1g	**14%**
Dietary Fiber 3.7g	**15%**
Sugars 32.9g	
Protein 6.9g	

Vitamin A 2%	•	Vitamin C 5%
Calcium 4%	•	Iron 7%

Nutrition Grade D-
* Based on a 2000 calorie diet

Ingredients
- 1/4 cup extra-virgin coconut oil, melted
- 1/2 cup raw honey
- 1/4 cup packed unrefined brown sugar
- 2 pasture-fed, free-range eggs
- 3 teaspoons pure vanilla extract
- 1 1/2 cups ripe bananas, mashed
- 1 3/4 cups almond flour
- 3 teaspoons baking soda
- 1 tablespoon cinnamon
- 1 cup walnuts, chopped
- 1/2 cup chocolate chips (70%-90% cocoa)

Directions
- **Preheat** oven to 350 degrees f. Line an 8-cup muffin pan with paper liners.
- **Whisk** together coconut oil, honey, and brown sugar in a bowl.

- **Beat** eggs in another bowl then stir in vanilla and mashed bananas. Mix together flour and baking soda then add to the egg mixture.
- **Stir** in cinnamon, walnuts, and chocolate chips. Fill muffin cups half full.
- **Bake** for 15-20 minutes, or until a toothpick inserted into the center of each muffin comes out clean or with only a few crumbs sticking to it.

14. Turkey Veggie Meatza

Servings: 4
Preparation time: 15 minutes
Cook time: 43 minutes
Ready in: 58 minutes

Nutrition Facts

Serving Size 263 g

Amount Per Serving

Calories 293   Calories from Fat 153

	% Daily Value*
Total Fat 17.0g	**26%**
Saturated Fat 6.9g	**34%**
Trans Fat 0.0g	
Cholesterol 229mg	**76%**
Sodium 592mg	**25%**
Total Carbohydrates 7.9g	**3%**
Dietary Fiber 2.3g	**9%**
Sugars 3.2g	
Protein 29.6g	

Vitamin A 67%	•	Vitamin C 75%
Calcium 7%	•	Iron 28%

Nutrition Grade B-
* Based on a 2000 calorie diet

Ingredients
- Olive oil for greasing
- 1 pound ground turkey
- 4 cloves garlic, crushed and chopped
- 1 tablespoon dried thyme
- 1 tablespoon dried basil
- 1/4 cup pure coconut milk
- 4 pasture-fed, free-range eggs
- 1/2 teaspoon garlic powder

- 1/2 teaspoon unrefined sea salt
- 1/2 teaspoon ground black pepper
- 1/2 cup zucchini, sliced
- 1/2 cup kalamata olives, chopped
- 1 1/2 cup mushrooms, sliced
- 1/2 cup roasted red peppers, chopped

Directions

- **Preheat** oven to 375 degrees f. Grease an 8×8 inch baking dish with olive oil.
- **Mix** together turkey, garlic, thyme, and basil in a bowl. Drain any excess oil from meat.
- **Bake** for 18 minutes, or until meat is just about cooked through.
- **Whisk** together coconut milk, eggs, garlic powder, salt, and pepper in a bowl.
- **Stir** in zucchini, kalamata olives, mushrooms, and roasted peppers.
- **Spread** the egg mixture on top of the meat crust. Return dish into the oven.
- **Bake** for 25-35 minutes, or until set. Cool then serve.

15. Carrot Walnuts Soufflé

Servings: 7
Preparation time: 10 minutes
Cook time: 45 minutes
Ready in: 55 minutes

Nutrition Facts

Serving Size 204 g

Amount Per Serving

Calories 382	Calories from Fat 229
	% Daily Value*
Total Fat 25.4g	**39%**
Saturated Fat 7.2g	**36%**
Trans Fat 0.0g	
Cholesterol 0mg	**0%**
Sodium 95mg	**4%**
Total Carbohydrates 33.2g	**11%**
Dietary Fiber 6.2g	**25%**
Sugars 24.3g	
Protein 11.3g	

Vitamin A 217%	•	Vitamin C 8%
Calcium 7%	•	Iron 9%

Nutrition Grade D+
* Based on a 2000 calorie diet

Ingredients
- 1 pounds carrots, chopped
- 1/3 cup organic coconut butter, melted
- 1/2 cup raw honey
- 3 tablespoons almond flour
- 1/4 teaspoon baking soda mixed with 1 1/2 teaspoon lemon juice
- 1 teaspoon pure vanilla extract
- 3 pasture-fed, free-range eggs, beaten
- 1 teaspoon ground cinnamon
- 1 teaspoon nutmeg
- 1 cup toasted walnuts, chopped

Directions
- **Preheat** oven to 350 degrees f (175 degrees c).
- **Add** carrots to a large pot of salted water. Cook for 15 minutes, or until tender; drain, cool, and mash.

- **Mix** mashed carrots with the remaining ingredients, except the walnuts. Transfer mixture to a 2-quart casserole dish. Spread walnuts evenly on top.
- **Bake** for 30 minutes.

16. Grain-free Granola

Servings: 8
Preparation time: 15 minutes
Cook time: 20-25 minutes
Ready in: 35 minutes

Nutrition Facts

Serving Size 75 g

Amount Per Serving

Calories 350   Calories from Fat 247

	% Daily Value*
Total Fat 27.4g	**42%**
Saturated Fat 9.6g	**48%**
Trans Fat 0.0g	
Cholesterol 0mg	**0%**
Sodium 246mg	**10%**
Total Carbohydrates 24.6g	**8%**
Dietary Fiber 3.7g	**15%**
Sugars 19.0g	
Protein 5.7g	

Vitamin A 1%	•	Vitamin C 3%
Calcium 4%	•	Iron 9%

Nutrition Grade D
* Based on a 2000 calorie diet

Ingredients
- 1 cup raw pecans
- 3/4 cup raw almonds
- 1/4 cup raw pumpkin seeds
- 1/4 cup raw unshelled sunflower seeds
- 1/4 cup unsweetened coconut flakes
- 1/2 cup raw honey (or pure maple syrup)
- 1/4 cup extra-virgin coconut oil
- 1/2 teaspoon ground cinnamon
- 1 teaspoon pure vanilla extract
- 1 cup dried cranberries
- 1 teaspoon unrefined sea salt

Directions

- **Preheat** oven to 275 degrees f. Line a baking sheet with parchment paper.
- **Combine** pecans, almonds, pumpkin seeds, sunflower seeds, and coconut flakes in a blender or food processor and process into smaller chunks.
- **Stir** together the honey, coconut oil, cinnamon, and vanilla in a medium bowl and heat in the microwave for 30 seconds. Stir in the nut mixture. Spread the mixture evenly onto the baking sheet.
- **Bake** mixture for about 20-25 minutes, or until lightly browned, stirring occasionally. Remove from oven and stir in the dried cranberries and salt.
- **Press** the mixture together to form a flat surface. Let cool then cut into chunks.

17. Walnut Banana Bread

Servings: 12
Preparation time: 10 minutes
Cook time: 1 hour
Ready in: 1 hour and 10 minutes

Nutrition Facts

Serving Size 94 g

Amount Per Serving

Calories 205   Calories from Fat 93

	% Daily Value*
Total Fat 10.4g	**16%**
Saturated Fat 4.1g	**20%**
Trans Fat 0.0g	
Cholesterol 13mg	**4%**
Sodium 156mg	**6%**
Total Carbohydrates 27.9g	**9%**
Dietary Fiber 1.9g	**8%**
Sugars 22.4g	
Protein 3.1g	

Vitamin A 1%	•	Vitamin C 6%
Calcium 2%	•	Iron 3%

Nutrition Grade D-

* Based on a 2000 calorie diet

Ingredients

- 4 ripe bananas, smashed

- 1/3 cup melted grass-fed raw milk butter, and 1 tablespoon for greasing (recommended: Organic Valley)
- 1 pasture-fed, free-range egg, beaten
- 1 teaspoon pure vanilla extract
- 3/4 cup raw honey
- 1 teaspoon ground cinnamon
- 1 teaspoon baking soda
- 1 dash unrefined sea salt
- 1 1/2 cups almond flour
- 1/2 cup toasted walnuts, chopped
  Directions
- **Preheat** oven to 350°f (175°c). Grease a 4x8 inch loaf pan with 1 tablespoon butter.
- **Combine** banana and 1/3 cup butter in a large bowl. Stir in egg, vanilla, honey, cinnamon, baking soda, and salt.
- **Add** the flour and mix well. Fold in chopped walnuts.
- **Bake** for 1 hour. Cool on a wire rack. Slice and serve.

18. Bacon 'n Veggie Quiche

Servings: 6
Preparation time: 15 minutes
Cook time: 15 minutes
Ready in: 30 minutes

Nutrition Facts

Serving Size 273 g

Amount Per Serving

Calories 155	Calories from Fat 95
	% Daily Value*
Total Fat 10.5g	**16%**
Saturated Fat 3.5g	**18%**
Trans Fat 0.0g	
Cholesterol 5mg	**2%**
Sodium 229mg	**10%**
Total Carbohydrates 1.9g	**1%**
Dietary Fiber 0.7g	**3%**
Sugars 0.8g	
Protein 12.8g	

Vitamin A 34%	•	Vitamin C 25%
Calcium 10%	•	Iron 3%

Nutrition Grade C
* Based on a 2000 calorie diet

Ingredients

- 6 slices nitrite/nitrate-free bacon
- Olive oil for greasing
- 8 pasture-fed, free-range eggs
- 1/2 cup onion, chopped
- 1/2 cup red bell pepper, diced
- 1/2 teaspoon unrefined sea salt
- 1/4 teaspoon ground black pepper
- 3 cups spinach leaves, chopped
- 6 tablespoons grass-fed raw milk parmesan cheese, shredded (recommended: Organic Valley)

Note: For strict Paleo version, omit cheese

Directions

- **Cook** the bacon for about 5 minutes in a large skillet over medium-high heat. Drain on paper towels.
- **Preheat** oven to 375 degrees f. Grease the cups of a 6-cup muffin pan with olive oil then line each cup with a slice of bacon.
- **Beat** together the eggs, onion, red bell pepper, salt, pepper, and spinach in a large bowl. Fill 3/4 of each muffin cup with the spinach mixture then sprinkle each with 1 tablespoon cheese on top.
- **Bake** for 10 to 14 minutes, or until set.

PALEO LUNCH

19. Cajun Chicken and Shrimp Jambalaya

Servings: 5
Preparation time: 30 minutes
Cook time: 25 minutes
Ready in: 55 minutes

Nutrition Facts

Serving Size 482 g

Amount Per Serving	
Calories 322	Calories from Fat 80
	% Daily Value*
Total Fat 8.9g	**14%**
Saturated Fat 1.9g	**10%**
Trans Fat 0.0g	
Cholesterol 84mg	**28%**
Sodium 1155mg	**48%**
Total Carbohydrates 30.2g	**10%**
Dietary Fiber 8.0g	**32%**
Sugars 14.1g	
Protein 34.2g	
Vitamin A 22% •	Vitamin C 90%
Calcium 16% •	Iron 22%

Nutrition Grade A
* Based on a 2000 calorie diet

Ingredients
- 1 tablespoon grass-fed raw milk butter (recommended: Organic Valley)
- 1 tablespoon olive oil
- 6 cloves garlic, finely chopped
- 1 large onion, diced
- 1 3/4 cups tomatoes, crushed
- 1/4 cup jalapenos, seeded and diced
- 2 teaspoons unrefined sea salt

- 1 teaspoon garlic powder
- 1 teaspoon onion powder
- 1 teaspoon dried thyme
- 1 teaspoon cayenne pepper
- 1 teaspoon paprika
- 1/2 teaspoon ground black pepper
- 1 cup low-sodium chicken broth
- 1 pound pasture-fed, free-range chicken breast, cooked, and chopped
- 1 pound peeled, deveined, and cooked shrimp
- 8 pods okra, sliced into rounds

Directions

- **Melt** butter in a large saucepan over medium heat then add the olive oil.
- **Sauté** garlic in butter and olive oil until lightly browned. Stir in the onions and cook for about 8 minutes, or until translucent.
- **Stir** in tomatoes and jalapenos. Combine salt, garlic powder, onion powder, thyme, cayenne pepper, paprika, and black pepper in a small bowl then sprinkle onto vegetables. Add the chicken broth to cover then bring mixture to a boil. Reduce heat to low.
- **Simmer** uncovered for 15 minutes, or until the mixture is thick. Add chicken, shrimp, and okra, simmer for 2 minutes until heated through.

20. Steak Salad Feast

Servings: 6
Ready in: 25 minutes

Nutrition Facts

Serving Size 390 g

Amount Per Serving

Calories 385 | Calories from Fat 232

	% Daily Value*
Total Fat 25.7g	**40%**
Saturated Fat 4.9g	**24%**
Trans Fat 0.0g	
Cholesterol 74mg	**25%**
Sodium 483mg	**20%**
Total Carbohydrates 11.9g	**4%**
Dietary Fiber 3.0g	**12%**
Sugars 6.8g	
Protein 28.0g	

Vitamin A 25%	•	Vitamin C 56%
Calcium 8%	•	Iron 87%

Nutrition Grade A-

* Based on a 2000 calorie diet

Ingredients

- 1 pound beef sirloin steak
- 6 plum tomatoes, sliced
- 8 cups romaine lettuce, torn into bite-size pieces
- 1/2 cup halved olives
- 1/2 cup fresh mushrooms, sliced
- 1/4 cup roasted sunflower seeds
- 1/2 cup crumbled grass-fed raw milk blue cheese (recommended: PastureLand Farmdog Blue)
- 1/4 cup almonds
- 1/3 cup olive oil
- 3 tablespoons balsamic vinegar
- 2 tablespoons lemon juice
- 1/2 teaspoon unrefined sea salt
- 1 pinch ground black pepper
- 3 teaspoons coconut aminos

  Note: For strict Paleo version, omit cheese

Directions

85

- **Broil** steak for 3 to 5 minutes each side. Cool, and then slice into bite-size pieces.
- **Arrange** the tomatoes, lettuce, olives, and mushrooms on chilled plates.
- **Top** salad with roasted sunflower seeds, blue cheese, almonds, and steak slices.
- **Stir** together the remaining ingredients in a small bowl then drizzle over salad.

21. Stir-Fried Beef with Flax seeds

Servings: 4
Preparation time: 40 minutes
Cook time: 9 minutes
Ready in: 49 minutes

Nutrition Facts

Serving Size 313 g

Amount Per Serving

Calories 320 Calories from Fat 198

% Daily Value*

Total Fat 22.1g	**34%**
Saturated Fat 3.1g	**15%**
Trans Fat 0.0g	
Cholesterol 0mg	**0%**
Sodium 184mg	**8%**
Total Carbohydrates 30.9g	**10%**
Dietary Fiber 3.8g	**15%**
Sugars 26.8g	
Protein 2.6g	

Vitamin A 52%	•	Vitamin C 173%
Calcium 3%	•	Iron 5%

Nutrition Grade B-

* Based on a 2000 calorie diet

Ingredients
- 4 tablespoons and 1 teaspoon olive oil
- 4 tablespoons coconut aminos
- 4 tablespoons raw honey
- 2 cloves garlic, minced
- 2 green onions, chopped
- 1/2 teaspoon red-pepper flakes
- 2 tablespoons flax seeds
- 1 pound beef stir-fry strips

- 2 red bell peppers, seeded and sliced thinly

Directions
- **Stir** together 4 tablespoons olive oil, coconut aminos, honey, garlic, green onions, and red pepper flakes in a large bowl. Add beef strips and toss well to coat.
- **Cover** and marinate in the fridge for at least 30 minutes, or overnight for best flavor.
- **Heat** 1 teaspoon olive oil in a wok. Add the bell peppers and stir-fry for 2 minutes, or until crisp-tender.
- **Add** the beef and marinade, cook for 5 minutes until beef is brown and sauce thickens. Stir in flax seeds and cook for additional 2 minutes.

22. Chicken Salad Surprise

Servings: 8
Ready in: 1 hour and 45 minutes

Nutrition Facts

Serving Size 176 g

Amount Per Serving

Calories 429   Calories from Fat 238

	% Daily Value*
Total Fat 26.4g	**41%**
Saturated Fat 4.6g	**23%**
Trans Fat 0.0g	
Cholesterol 86mg	**29%**
Sodium 169mg	**7%**
Total Carbohydrates 26.9g	**9%**
Dietary Fiber 3.1g	**12%**
Sugars 17.3g	
Protein 24.8g	

Vitamin A 7%	•	Vitamin C 17%
Calcium 5%	•	Iron 13%

Nutrition Grade B+
* Based on a 2000 calorie diet

Ingredients
- 1 large pasture-fed, free-range egg
- 1 1/2 tablespoons apple cider vinegar
- 1/2 teaspoon Dijon mustard

- 1/2 cup avocado oil
- 1/2 cup olive oil
- 1/4 teaspoon unrefined sea salt
- 1/4 teaspoon ground white pepper
- 4 cups cooked pasture-fed, free-range chicken breast fillet, cubed
- 1/2 cup almonds, chopped
- 1 1/2 cups raisins
- 1 cup celery, chopped
- 1/2 cup halved cashews
- 1/2 cup red bell pepper, minced
- 2 green onions, chopped
- 1/4 teaspoon ground black pepper
- 1/2 teaspoon unrefined sea salt

Directions

- **Prepare** the Paleo mayonnaise: combine egg, cider vinegar, and mustard in a blender, and blend until frothy. Add the avocado oil and olive oil, drop by drop, until smooth and creamy. Season with 1/4 teaspoon salt, and white pepper. Place in a sealed container and refrigerate for 30 minutes.
- **Toss** together the prepared mayonnaise and the remaining ingredients. Chill for at least 1 hour and serve.

23. Beef Veggie Soup

Servings: 5
Preparation time: 15 minutes
Cook time: 25 minutes
Ready in: 40 minutes

Nutrition Facts

Serving Size 336 g

Amount Per Serving

Calories 235	Calories from Fat 57

	% Daily Value*
Total Fat 6.3g	**10%**
Saturated Fat 2.3g	**11%**
Trans Fat 0.0g	
Cholesterol 81mg	**27%**
Sodium 813mg	**34%**
Total Carbohydrates 13.2g	**4%**
Dietary Fiber 2.7g	**11%**
Sugars 9.8g	
Protein 31.0g	

Vitamin A 81%	•	Vitamin C 17%
Calcium 3%	•	Iron 105%

Nutrition Grade A
* Based on a 2000 calorie diet

Ingredients
- 1 pound lean ground beef
- 1/2 cup onion, chopped
- 2 cups organic tomato sauce
- 1/2 cup celery, chopped
- 1 cup carrots, sliced
- 1-1/4 cups mushrooms, chopped
- 1-1/4 cups low sodium beef broth
- 1 tablespoon coconut amino
- 1 tablespoon raw honey

Directions
- **Place** a large skillet over medium heat. Add beef and onion, cook until meat is no longer pink and drain.
- **Add** the remaining ingredients and bring to a boil; stirring occasionally.
- **Turn** heat to low. Simmer covered for 10 minutes or until bubbly.

24. Cajun Turkey and Rice

Servings: 6
Preparation time: 15 minutes
Cook time: 1 hour and 10 minutes
Ready in: 1 hour 25 minutes

```
Nutrition Facts
Serving Size 312 g

Amount Per Serving
Calories 330              Calories from Fat 127
                                   % Daily Value*
Total Fat 14.1g                              22%
  Saturated Fat 3.9g                         20%
  Trans Fat 0.0g
Cholesterol 82mg                             27%
Sodium 693mg                                 29%
Total Carbohydrates 25.0g                     8%
  Dietary Fiber 4.6g                         18%
  Sugars 7.1g
Protein 26.5g

Vitamin A 7%          •          Vitamin C 92%
Calcium 14%           •              Iron 21%

Nutrition Grade B+
* Based on a 2000 calorie diet
```

Ingredients
- 1 tablespoon olive oil
- 2 cloves garlic, minced
- 1 onion, chopped
- 1 pound ground turkey
- 1 1/4 cups tomatoes, diced
- 1 cup organic tomato sauce
- 1/2 cup gluten-free long grain rice, uncooked
- 1 teaspoon unrefined sea salt
- 1/4 teaspoon ground black pepper
- 1/2 teaspoon dried basil
- 1/4 teaspoon ground cumin
- 1/4 teaspoon ground cayenne pepper
- 1 head cabbage, chopped
- 1/2 cup grass-fed raw milk parmesan cheese, shredded (recommended: Organic Valley)

Note: For strict Paleo version, omit cheese and go for Cauliflower Rice (see Recipe No. 55) instead of long-grain rice

Directions

- **Preheat** oven to 350 degrees f.
- **Heat** olive oil in a large skillet over medium heat. Add garlic and sauté until lightly browned. Add onion and meat, cook for 8 minutes or until meat is no longer pink. Discard liquid from skillet.
- **Add** the tomatoes, tomato sauce, and rice; season with salt, pepper, dried basil, cumin, and cayenne pepper.
- **Spread** mixture into a 9x12-inch baking pan. Sprinkle cabbage and cheese over the top.
- **Bake** covered for 1 hour and 10 minutes, or until the rice is tender.

25. Zucchini Patties

Servings: 3
Preparation time: 15 minutes
Cook time: 10 minutes
Ready in: 25 minutes

Nutrition Facts

Serving Size 221 g

Amount Per Serving

Calories 243 — Calories from Fat 175

	% Daily Value*
Total Fat 19.5g	**30%**
Saturated Fat 5.1g	**26%**
Trans Fat 0.0g	
Cholesterol 122mg	**41%**
Sodium 284mg	**12%**
Total Carbohydrates 5.8g	**2%**
Dietary Fiber 1.7g	**7%**
Sugars 2.1g	
Protein 12.6g	

Vitamin A 11%	•	Vitamin C 25%
Calcium 28%	•	Iron 6%

Nutrition Grade C+

* Based on a 2000 calorie diet

Ingredients

- 2 eggs, beaten
- 2 cups grated zucchini

- 1/2 cup grass-fed raw milk Parmesan cheese, grated (recommended: Organic Valley)
- 1/4 cup onion, chopped
- 1/2 cup almond flour
- 3 cloves garlic, crushed
- 1 roasted red bell peppers, finely diced
- 3/4 teaspoon unrefined sea salt
- 1/2 teaspoon red pepper flakes
- 2 tablespoons olive oil

Note: For strict Paleo version, omit cheese

Directions

- **Combine** all ingredients (except the olive oil) in a bowl.

- **Heat** olive oil in a skillet over medium-high heat. Drop zucchini mixture by tablespoon and brown for 3 minutes on each side.

- **Drain** on paper towels, cool and serve.

26. Easy Spinach 'n Mushroom Frittata

Servings: 2
Preparation time: 15 minutes
Cook time: 30 minutes
Ready in: 45 minutes

Nutrition Facts

Serving Size 387 g

Amount Per Serving

Calories 240	Calories from Fat 106
	% Daily Value*
Total Fat 11.7g	**18%**
Saturated Fat 4.3g	**22%**
Trans Fat 0.0g	
Cholesterol 335mg	**112%**
Sodium 840mg	**35%**
Total Carbohydrates 17.0g	**6%**
Dietary Fiber 6.4g	**26%**
Sugars 5.8g	
Protein 20.9g	

Vitamin A 465%	•	Vitamin C 94%
Calcium 32%	•	Iron 39%

Nutrition Grade A
* Based on a 2000 calorie diet

Ingredients

- Olive oil for greasing
- 4 eggs
- 1 (10 ounce) package frozen chopped spinach, thawed
- 1 cup carrot, diced
- 1/2 cup grape tomatoes, diced
- 1/4 cup grass-fed raw milk Parmesan cheese, freshly grated (recommended: Organic Valley)
- 3/4 cup Portobello mushrooms, chopped
- 1/2 cup scallions, finely chopped
- 1 teaspoon garlic powder
- 1/2 teaspoon dried thyme
- 1/4 teaspoon dried rosemary
- 1/4 teaspoon basil
- 1/2 teaspoon unrefined sea salt
- 1 pinch ground black pepper

Note: For strict Paleo version, omit cheese

Directions

- **Preheat** oven to 375 degrees F. Grease a 9-inch pie plate with olive oil.
- **Mix** all ingredients in the pie plate.
- **Bake** for 30 minutes, or until set. Cool, and cut in wedges to serve.

27. Cheddar Pear Salad with Caramelized Pecans

Servings: 16
Preparation time: 20 minutes
Cook time: 5 minutes
Ready in: 25 minutes

Nutrition Facts

Serving Size 115 g

Amount Per Serving

Calories 368   Calories from Fat 116

	% Daily Value*
Total Fat 12.9g	**20%**
Saturated Fat 2.8g	**14%**
Trans Fat 0.0g	
Cholesterol 8mg	**3%**
Sodium 108mg	**5%**
Total Carbohydrates 40.7g	**14%**
Dietary Fiber 14.4g	**58%**
Sugars 9.4g	
Protein 15.9g	

Vitamin A 1126%	Vitamin C 191%
Calcium 31%	Iron 79%

Nutrition Grade B+
* Based on a 2000 calorie diet

Ingredients

- 3 pears, peeled, cored and chopped
- 5 ounces grass-fed raw milk Cheddar cheese, crumbled (recommended: Organic Pastures or PastureLand True Raw Milk Cheddar)
- 1 head lettuce leaves, torn into bite-size pieces
- 1 cup cashew halves
- 1/2 cup red onion, thinly sliced
- 1 clove garlic, chopped
- 1 1/2 teaspoons Dijon mustard
- 1/2 teaspoon unrefined sea salt
- 1/4 teaspoon fresh ground black pepper
- 1/3 cup extra virgin olive oil
- 3 tablespoons apple cider vinegar
- 1/4 cup and 1 1/2 teaspoons raw honey
- 1/2 cup pecans

- 1/4 teaspoon ground cinnamon

Note: For strict Paleo version, omit cheese

Directions
- **Stir** together garlic, mustard, salt, pepper, olive oil, cider vinegar, and 1 1/2 teaspoons honey in a small bowl.
- **Combine** pears, cheese, lettuce, cashews, and onions in a large bowl then drizzle with the vinegar mixture.
- **Toss** well to coat.
- **Stir** together 1/4 cup honey, cinnamon, and pecans in a skillet over medium heat until caramelized, about 5 minutes. Cool pecans onto parchment paper, and break into pieces.
- **Top** salad with the caramelized pecans.

28. Lime Chicken Picante with Steamed Carrots and Cauliflower

Servings: 6
Preparation time: 20 minutes
Cook time: 37 minutes
Ready in: 57 minutes

Nutrition Facts

Serving Size 270 g

Amount Per Serving

Calories 227	Calories from Fat 67

	% Daily Value*
Total Fat 7.4g	**11%**
Saturated Fat 1.2g	**6%**
Trans Fat 0.0g	
Cholesterol 66mg	**22%**
Sodium 636mg	**26%**
Total Carbohydrates 11.1g	**4%**
Dietary Fiber 3.1g	**13%**
Sugars 4.9g	
Protein 24.8g	

Vitamin A 207%	•	Vitamin C 48%
Calcium 43%	•	Iron 4%

Nutrition Grade C+
* Based on a 2000 calorie diet

Ingredients
- 1/4 cup Dijon mustard

- 2 tablespoons fresh lime juice
- 1/2 cup organic low-sodium chunky salsa
- 6 (4-ounce) skinless, boneless pasture-fed, free-range chicken breasts
- 2 tablespoons extra-virgin olive oil
- 1 lime, sliced into 6 wedges
- 6 carrots, cut into 1/2-inch rounds
- 1 head cauliflower, cut into bite-size florets
- 1/4 teaspoon unrefined sea salt

Directions

- **Stir** together the mustard, lime juice, and salsa in a large bowl. Add chicken and coat with the salsa mixture. Cover, and place in the fridge to marinate for at least 30 minutes.
- **Heat** olive oil in a large skillet over medium heat. Add the marinated chicken and brown on all sides.
- **Boil** marinade in a saucepan for 5 minutes then pour over chicken.
- **Sauté** chicken for another 3 to 5 minutes or until marinade starts to glaze.
- **Place** chicken onto individual plates; spooning marinade over chicken.
- **Place** a steamer in a large saucepan of boiling water. Add the vegetables and steam covered for about 7 minutes, or until tender.
- **Transfer** vegetables to a bowl and season with 1/4 teaspoon salt. Cover to keep warm.
- **Top** each breast with 1 lime wedge and place steamed vegetables on the side.

29. Holiday Apple and Sunflower Seed Salad

Servings: 4
Ready in: 25 minutes

Nutrition Facts

Serving Size 322 g

Amount Per Serving

Calories 372	Calories from Fat 251

% Daily Value*

Total Fat 27.9g	**43%**
Saturated Fat 3.4g	**17%**
Trans Fat 0.0g	
Cholesterol 0mg	**0%**
Sodium 505mg	**21%**
Total Carbohydrates 26.2g	**9%**
Dietary Fiber 6.0g	**24%**
Sugars 12.4g	
Protein 10.2g	

Vitamin A 112%	•	Vitamin C 102%
Calcium 12%	•	Iron 19%

Nutrition Grade B
* Based on a 2000 calorie diet

Ingredients

- 2 green apples - washed, cored and cubed
- 1/2 cup roasted sunflower seeds
- 1/2 cup sliced walnuts
- 1/2 cup halved olives
- 5 oz. mixed baby kale leaves, chopped
- 2 tomatoes, diced
  Dressing:
- 1 pasture-fed, free-range egg
- 1/2 tablespoon apple cider vinegar
- 1/8 teaspoon Dijon mustard
- 2 tablespoons avocado oil
- 2 tablespoons olive oil
- 1/8 teaspoon unrefined sea salt
- 1/8 teaspoon ground white pepper
- 1/4 cup balsamic vinaigrette
- 4 tablespoons pure full-fat coconut milk
- 2 tablespoons fresh dill, finely minced

- 1 teaspoon garlic powder
- 1 teaspoon apple cider vinegar
- 1/2 teaspoon unrefined sea salt
- 1/4 teaspoon freshly ground black pepper

Directions
- **Combine** apples, sunflower seeds, walnuts, olives, kale, and tomatoes in a large bowl.
- **Prepare** the Paleo mayonnaise: Place egg, 1/2 tablespoon cider vinegar, and mustard in a blender, and blend until frothy. Add the avocado oil and olive oil, drop by drop, until smooth and creamy. Season with 1/8 teaspoon salt and white pepper. Place in a sealed container and refrigerate for 15 minutes.
- **Stir** together the prepared mayonnaise and the remaining dressing ingredients in a small bowl then pour over salad and toss well.

30. Shredded Brussels Sprouts with Bacon

Servings: 5
Preparation time: 10 minutes
Cook time: 10-15 minutes
Ready in: 20 minutes

Nutrition Facts

Serving Size 275 g

Amount Per Serving

Calories 378	Calories from Fat 232

	% Daily Value*
Total Fat 25.8g	**40%**
Saturated Fat 2.4g	**12%**
Cholesterol 0mg	**0%**
Sodium 236mg	**10%**
Total Carbohydrates 25.7g	**9%**
Dietary Fiber 8.1g	**33%**
Sugars 9.2g	
Protein 17.7g	

Vitamin A 30%	•	Vitamin C 261%
Calcium 9%	•	Iron 22%

Nutrition Grade A
* Based on a 2000 calorie diet

Ingredients

- 1/2 pound lean, nitrate/nitrite-free sliced bacon
- 1/4 cup olive oil
- 1 clove garlic, thinly sliced
- 1 medium shallot, finely chopped
- 2/3 cup pine nuts
- 2 pounds Brussels sprouts, cored and shredded
- 3 green onions, minced
- 1/2 teaspoon unrefined sea salt
- 1/2 teaspoon ground black pepper
- 1/4 cup raisins

Directions

- **Cook** bacon in a large skillet medium-high heat until crisp.
- **Drain** bacon in paper towels and discard grease. Crumble and set aside.
- **Heat** olive oil in the same skillet over medium heat. Add garlic and shallot and sauté until shallot is translucent.
- **Stir** in pine nuts and cook until browned. Add brussels sprouts and green onions to the pan, season with salt and pepper.
- **Cook** for 10 to 15 minutes, or until sprouts are wilted and tender.
- **Stir** in crumbled bacon and raisins.

31. Lamb and Vegetable Stew

Servings: 6
Preparation time: 15 minutes
Cook time: 20 minutes
Ready in: 35 minutes

Nutrition Facts

Serving Size 384 g

Amount Per Serving

Calories 304	Calories from Fat 116
	% Daily Value*
Total Fat 12.9g	**20%**
Saturated Fat 3.1g	**16%**
Trans Fat 0.0g	
Cholesterol 104mg	**35%**
Sodium 335mg	**14%**
Total Carbohydrates 11.2g	**4%**
Dietary Fiber 3.4g	**13%**
Sugars 4.9g	
Protein 33.7g	

Vitamin A 148%	•	Vitamin C 36%
Calcium 16%	•	Iron 15%

Nutrition Grade C+

* Based on a 2000 calorie diet

Ingredients

- 1 1/2 pounds boneless lamb steaks, cut into 2-inch pieces
- 1 tablespoon fresh thyme, chopped
- 1 teaspoon unrefined sea salt
- 1 clove garlic, chopped
- 1/2 teaspoon ground black pepper
- 1 bay leaf
- 2 tablespoons olive oil, divided
- 4 carrots, cut into 3-inch sticks
- 1 onion, thinly sliced
- 1 tablespoon almond flour
- 1/2 cup dry white wine
- 2 cups organic low-sodium beef broth
- 1 3/4 cup diced tomatoes
- 1 cup celery, sliced
- 1/2 cup fresh parsley leaves, chopped

Directions

- **Season** lamb with thyme, 1/2 teaspoon salt, garlic, 1/4 teaspoon pepper, and bay leaf.
- **Heat** 1 tablespoon of olive oil in a large saucepan over medium-high heat. Cook lamb in oil for 6 to 8 minutes, or until browned all both sides. Set aside.
- **Add** the carrots and onion to the saucepan then drizzle with remaining olive oil. Cook for 3 minutes, until vegetable starts to soften. Stir in the flour and wine, simmer for 1 minute.
- **Pour** in beef broth then add tomatoes, and celery; simmer for 8 to 10 minutes, or until the vegetables are tender.
- **Add** the lamb then season with remaining salt and pepper. Remove the bay leaf.
- **Serve** warm topped with chopped parsley.

32. Fried Lemon Cod and Brown Rice

Servings: 8
Preparation time: 15 minutes
Cook time: 1 hour and 10 minutes
Ready in: 1 hour and 25 minutes

Nutrition Facts

Serving Size 265 g

Amount Per Serving

Calories 291	Calories from Fat 68
	% Daily Value*
Total Fat 7.6g	12%
Saturated Fat 1.1g	5%
Cholesterol 42mg	14%
Sodium 389mg	16%
Total Carbohydrates 36.8g	12%
Dietary Fiber 2.3g	9%
Protein 19.4g	

Vitamin A 1%	•	Vitamin C 7%
Calcium 1%	•	Iron 23%

Nutrition Grade A-
* Based on a 2000 calorie diet

Ingredients

- 1 1/2 pounds cod fillets

- 1 lemon, juiced
- 2 cloves garlic, finely chopped
- 1/2 teaspoon unrefined sea salt
- 1/2 teaspoon ground black pepper
- 3 tablespoons extra-virgin olive oil
- 3 tablespoons cilantro, chopped
  Brown Rice:
- 2 cups long-grain gluten-free brown rice
- 4 cups water
- 1 teaspoon unrefined sea salt
  Note: For strict Paleo version, go for Cauliflower Rice (see Recipe No. 55) instead of Brown Rice

Directions
- **Rinse** brown rice under cold water.
- **Boil** brown rice in a pot of water over high heat; stir in the salt. Reduce the heat to low. Cover the pot and simmer for 45 to 50 minutes, or until the rice is tender. Remove pan from heat, cover and let sit for 10 minutes more.
- **Drizzle** fillets with lemon juice then sprinkle with garlic, salt, and pepper.
- **Heat** olive oil in a large skillet over medium high heat.
- **Add** fillets and cook for 4 minutes each side, or until flaky. Sprinkle chopped cilantro over the top then serve fried cod fillets over brown rice.

33. Spicy Mongolian Beef

Servings: 5
Preparation time: 1hour and 15 minutes
Cook time: 8 minutes
Ready in: 1 hour 23 minutes

Nutrition Facts

Serving Size 170 g

Amount Per Serving

Calories 259	Calories from Fat 103

	% Daily Value*
Total Fat 11.5g	**18%**
Saturated Fat 4.9g	**25%**
Trans Fat 0.0g	
Cholesterol 81mg	**27%**
Sodium 88mg	**4%**
Total Carbohydrates 9.7g	**3%**
Dietary Fiber 1.9g	**7%**
Sugars 6.0g	
Protein 28.5g	

Vitamin A 107%	•	Vitamin C 59%
Calcium 2%	•	Iron 98%

Nutrition Grade B-
* Based on a 2000 calorie diet

Ingredients

- 1 pound beef flank steak, trimmed and thinly sliced
- 1/3 cup coconut amino
- 1 tablespoon sesame oil
- 1 teaspoon red wine
- 1 tablespoon raw honey
- 1 tablespoon garlic, minced
- 2 teaspoons fresh ginger, minced
- 1 tablespoon red pepper flakes
- 1 tablespoon coconut oil
- 2 carrots, thinly sliced
- 2 large green onions, thinly sliced
- 1 red bell pepper, finely chopped

Directions

- **Place** beef in a large bowl.

- **Combine** coconut amino, sesame oil, red wine, honey, garlic, ginger, and red pepper flakes in a small bowl. Pour mixture over beef and toss well. Cover, and place in the fridge to marinate for 1 hour, or overnight for best flavor.
- **Heat** coconut oil in a wok over high heat. Add the carrots, green onions, and red bell pepper, cook for 1 minute.
- **Stir** in the beef and marinade, cook for 5 minutes, or until sauce thickens.

34. Bacon Spinach Salad

Servings: 8
Preparation time: 15 minutes
Cook time: 10 minutes
Ready in: 25 minutes

Nutrition Facts

Serving Size 185 g

Amount Per Serving

Calories 371	Calories from Fat 232
	% Daily Value*
Total Fat 25.8g	**40%**
Saturated Fat 3.5g	**18%**
Trans Fat 0.0g	
Cholesterol 61mg	**20%**
Sodium 353mg	**15%**
Total Carbohydrates 28.3g	**9%**
Dietary Fiber 2.4g	**10%**
Sugars 24.4g	
Protein 10.9g	

Vitamin A 108%	•	Vitamin C 29%
Calcium 9%	•	Iron 13%

Nutrition Grade B+
* Based on a 2000 calorie diet

Ingredients
- 1/2 pound lean nitrite/nitrate-free bacon.
- 1 pound spinach, rinsed and chopped
- 1/4 cup sliced fresh mushrooms
- 3 boiled eggs, peeled and chopped
- 1/2 cup sliced almonds
- 1 onion, chopped
- 1 teaspoon sesame seed

- 1/2 cup extra-virgin olive oil
- 2/3 cup raw honey
- 1/3 cup balsamic vinegar
- 1 tablespoon prepared Dijon-style mustard
- 1 teaspoon sea salt
- 1/2 teaspoon ground black pepper

Directions

- **Cook** bacon in a large skillet over medium high heat until browned. Drain bacon in paper towels then crumble and place in a large bowl.\
- **Add** the spinach, mushrooms, eggs, and almonds.
- **Place** the onion, sesame seed, olive oil, honey, vinegar, mustard, salt, and pepper in a blender; blend until smooth.
- **Pour** dressing over salad, gently toss to coat then serve.

35. Thai-style Shrimp Coconut Soup

Servings: 8
Preparation time: 15 minutes
Cook time: 23 minutes
Ready in: 38 minutes

Nutrition Facts

Serving Size 292 g

Amount Per Serving

Calories 317	Calories from Fat 244
	% Daily Value*
Total Fat 27.1g	**42%**
Saturated Fat 22.5g	**112%**
Cholesterol 84mg	**28%**
Sodium 594mg	**25%**
Total Carbohydrates 9.6g	**3%**
Dietary Fiber 2.5g	**10%**
Sugars 5.2g	
Protein 13.0g	

Vitamin A 1%	•	Vitamin C 8%
Calcium 3%	•	Iron 20%

Nutrition Grade C+

* Based on a 2000 calorie diet

Ingredients

- 2 teaspoons olive oil
- 3 cloves garlic, minced
- 1 1/2 tablespoons grated fresh ginger
- 1 1/2 teaspoons red chili paste
- 3/4 cup fresh mushrooms, sliced
- 1 stalk lemongrass, minced
- 3 cups low-sodium chicken broth
- 3 tablespoons low-sodium fish sauce
- 2 teaspoons raw honey
- 3 1/2 cups pure light coconut milk
- 3/4 pound medium shrimp - peeled and deveined
- 2 tablespoons fresh lime juice
- 1/2 teaspoon sea salt
- 1/4 cup chopped fresh cilantro

Directions

- **Heat** olive oil in a large pot over medium heat.
- **Add** the garlic, ginger, chili paste, mushrooms, and lemongrass and cook for 3 minutes.
- **Stir** in chicken broth, fish sauce, honey, and coconut milk over the mixture; bring to a simmer for 15 minutes.
- **Add** the shrimp and cook for 5 minutes, until no longer translucent.
- **Stir** in the lime juice and salt. Sprinkle cilantro on top.

36. Salmon Salad

Servings: 3
Ready in: 15 minutes

```
Nutrition Facts
Serving Size 246 g

Amount Per Serving
Calories 368              Calories from Fat 239
                               % Daily Value*
Total Fat 26.5g                           41%
  Saturated Fat 5.0g                      25%
  Trans Fat 0.0g
Cholesterol 71mg                          24%
Sodium 585mg                              24%
Total Carbohydrates 3.6g                   1%
  Dietary Fiber 1.6g                       7%
  Sugars 1.6g
Protein 28.5g

Vitamin A 10%          •        Vitamin C 19%
Calcium 5%             •              Iron 5%

Nutrition Grade B
* Based on a 2000 calorie diet
```

Ingredients

- 12 ounces pink salmon
- 2 cups shredded lettuce leaves
- 1/2 cup celery, finely chopped
- 3/4 teaspoon lemon juice
- 3/4 teaspoon dried basil
- 3/4 teaspoon sea salt
- 1/2 cup green onions, finely sliced
  Paleo Mayonnaise:
- 1 pasture-fed, free-range egg
- 1/2 tablespoon lemon juice
- 1/8 teaspoon Dijon mustard
- 2 tablespoons avocado oil
- 2 tablespoons olive oil
- 1/8 teaspoon unrefined sea salt
- 1/8 teaspoon ground white pepper

Directions

- **Place** salmon, lettuce, and celery in a medium bowl.
- **Prepare** the Paleo mayonnaise: combine egg, lemon juice, and mustard in a blender, and blend until frothy. Add the avocado oil and olive oil, drop by drop, until smooth and creamy. Season with salt and white pepper. Place in a sealed container and refrigerate for 15 minutes.
- **Stir** together the prepared mayonnaise and the remaining ingredients (except the green onions) in a small bowl then toss with the salad.
- **Sprinkle** green onions over the top. Chill and serve.

PALEO DINNER

37. Shrimp Stir-fry with Mushrooms and Zucchini

Servings: 4
Preparation time: 15 minutes
Cook time: 8 minutes
Ready in: 23 minutes

Nutrition Facts

Serving Size 250 g

Amount Per Serving

Calories 212   Calories from Fat 66

% Daily Value*

Total Fat 7.3g	**11%**
Saturated Fat 1.4g	**7%**
Trans Fat 0.0g	
Cholesterol 239mg	**80%**
Sodium 440mg	**18%**
Total Carbohydrates 8.1g	**3%**
Dietary Fiber 0.9g	**4%**
Sugars 2.3g	
Protein 27.3g	

Vitamin A 11%	•	Vitamin C 13%
Calcium 12%	•	Iron 7%

Nutrition Grade B-

* Based on a 2000 calorie diet

Ingredients
- 1 pound shrimp, peeled and deveined
- 1 1/2 tablespoon olive oil
- 2 tablespoons garlic, minced
- 1 teaspoon fresh ginger root, minced
- 1 cup mushrooms, sliced
- 1 cup diced zucchini
- 1/2 cup chopped celery

- 2 tablespoons green onions, chopped
- 1/4 teaspoon unrefined sea salt
- 1/3 cup low-sodium chicken broth
- 2 teaspoons white wine
- 1 1/2 teaspoons coconut amino
- 1 1/2 teaspoons arrowroot powder
- 3/4 teaspoon raw honey
- 1/4 teaspoon crushed red pepper flakes
- 1 pinch ground black pepper

Directions

- **Soak** shrimp in a large bowl of salted water for 5 minutes. Rinse shrimps, and dry on paper towels.
- **Heat** 1 tablespoon olive oil in a large skillet over high heat. Add shrimp and cook for 1 minute or until pink on all sides, turning constantly.
- **Add** 1/2 tablespoon olive oil to the skillet then stir in garlic, ginger, mushrooms, zucchini, celery, green onions, and salt; stir-fry for about 1 minute or until tender.
- **Mix** the chicken broth, white wine, coconut amino, arrowroot powder, honey, red pepper flakes, and black pepper in a small bowl then stir mixture into skillet; cook until sauce thickens. Serve warm.

38. Baked Maple Salmon

Servings: 4
Preparation time: 40 minutes
Cook time: 20 minutes
Ready in: 1 hour

Nutrition Facts

Serving Size 187 g

Amount Per Serving

Calories 291   Calories from Fat 127

	% Daily Value*
Total Fat 14.1g	**22%**
Saturated Fat 2.8g	**14%**
Trans Fat 0.0g	
Cholesterol 71mg	**24%**
Sodium 246mg	**10%**
Total Carbohydrates 14.5g	**5%**
Sugars 11.8g	
Protein 25.3g	

Vitamin A 4%	•	Vitamin C 12%
Calcium 4%	•	Iron 4%

Nutrition Grade B+

* Based on a 2000 calorie diet

Ingredients

- 1 pound salmon
- 1/4 cup pure maple syrup
- 2 tablespoons coconut amino
- 2 cloves garlic, minced
- 1/4 teaspoon garlic powder
- 1/4 teaspoon sea salt
- 1/8 teaspoon ground black pepper
- 2 tablespoons parsley, chopped

Directions

- **Place** salmon in a shallow baking dish.
- **Stir** together the maple syrup, coconut amino, minced garlic, garlic powder, salt, pepper, and parsley in a small bowl then pour over salmon.
- **Cover** and marinate salmon for 30 minutes in the fridge; turn once to coat.

- **Preheat** oven to 400 degrees f.
- **Bake** salmon uncovered for 20 minutes or until salmon flakes easily with a fork.

39. Beef Bolognese Stuffed Bell Peppers

Servings: 6
Preparation time: 30 minutes
Cook time: 1 hour and 5 minutes
Ready in: 1 hour 35 minutes

Nutrition Facts

Serving Size 303 g

Amount Per Serving

Calories 346	Calories from Fat 138

	% Daily Value*
Total Fat 15.3g	**24%**
Saturated Fat 3.8g	**19%**
Trans Fat 0.0g	
Cholesterol 55mg	**18%**
Sodium 260mg	**11%**
Total Carbohydrates 28.1g	**9%**
Dietary Fiber 5.1g	**20%**
Sugars 9.7g	
Protein 23.4g	

Vitamin A 93%	Vitamin C 282%
Calcium 9%	Iron 72%

Nutrition Grade B+

* Based on a 2000 calorie diet

Ingredients

- 1/2 cup uncooked gluten-free brown rice
- 2 tablespoons olive oil, divided
- 1 clove garlic, minced
- 1/8 cup carrots, minced
- 1/8 cup onions, diced
- 3/4 pound ground beef
- 1 1/2 cups stewed tomatoes
- 1/2 cup tomato paste
- 2 tablespoons fresh parsley, chopped
- 1 clove garlic, minced
- 1/2 teaspoon dried oregano
- 2 tablespoons olive oil
- 1 onion, finely diced
- 1/4 cup red wine

- 1/2 teaspoon red pepper flakes
- 1/2 teaspoon unrefined sea salt
- 1/4 teaspoon ground black pepper
- 1/2 cup grated grass-fed raw milk Parmesan cheese, divided (recommended: Organic Valley)
- 3 red bell peppers, seeded and halved lengthwise
- 3 green bell peppers, seeded and halved lengthwise
  Note: For strict Paleo version, omit cheese and go for Cauliflower Rice (see Recipe No. 55, no need to cook) instead of brown rice

Directions

- **Boil** water in a saucepan over medium heat. Stir in rice then reduce heat. Simmer covered for 20 minutes, or until rice is tender and fluffy; set aside.
- **Heat** 1 tablespoon of olive oil in a large skillet over medium high heat. Stir in garlic, onions and carrots and cook until tender. Add ground beef and cook until browned; drain off any excess liquid.
- **Stir** together the tomatoes, tomato paste, parsley, garlic, oregano, olive oil, onion, red wine, red pepper flakes, salt, and pepper in a bowl. Pour mixture over beef in the saucepan then simmer for 10 minutes. Stir in cooked rice and 1/4 cup parmesan cheese and simmer for 5 minutes more.
- **Preheat** oven to 375 degrees f.
- **Fill** each bell pepper with the beef mixture then drizzle with remaining olive oil and top with remaining parmesan cheese. Place bell peppers in a shallow baking dish.
- **Bake** for 30 minutes.

40. Spinach and Mushrooms Stuffed Chicken Breasts

Servings: 4
Preparation time: 45 minutes
Cook time: 1 hour
Ready in: 1 hour and 45 minutes

Nutrition Facts

Serving Size 289 g

Amount Per Serving

Calories 348   Calories from Fat 173

	% Daily Value*
Total Fat 19.2g	**30%**
Saturated Fat 3.5g	**18%**
Trans Fat 0.0g	
Cholesterol 137mg	**46%**
Sodium 635mg	**26%**
Total Carbohydrates 8.6g	**3%**
Dietary Fiber 2.8g	**11%**
Sugars 2.8g	
Protein 33.2g	

Vitamin A 73%	•	Vitamin C 32%
Calcium 7%	•	Iron 10%

Nutrition Grade C+

* Based on a 2000 calorie diet

Ingredients

- 1 pasture-fed, free-range egg yolk
- 2 teaspoons lemon juice
- 1/4 teaspoon Dijon mustard
- 1/4 cup avocado oil
- 1/4 cup olive oil
- 1/4 teaspoon unrefined sea salt
- 1/4 teaspoon ground white pepper
- 5 cups fresh spinach leaves, chopped
- 1 cup mushrooms, chopped
- 1/4 cup crumbled grass-fed raw milk feta cheese (recommended: Farmstead Fresh or Oliver Farms)
- 2 cloves garlic, chopped
- 2 onions, chopped
- 1/2 teaspoon unrefined sea salt
- 1/4 teaspoon freshly ground black pepper

- 4 skinless, boneless pasture-fed, free-range chicken breasts, butterflied
  Note: For strict Paleo version, omit cheese

Directions
- **Preheat** oven to 375 degrees F (190 degrees C).
- **Prepare** the Paleo mayonnaise: combine egg, lemon juice, and mustard in a blender, and blend until frothy. Add the avocado oil and olive oil, drop by drop, until smooth and creamy. Season with 1/4 teaspoon salt, and white pepper. Place in a sealed container and refrigerate for 30 minutes.
- **Combine** the spinach, mushrooms, paleo mayonnaise, cheese, garlic, onions, salt, and pepper in a bowl.
- **Spoon** spinach mixture into chicken breasts and secure with toothpicks.
- **Place** stuffed chicken breasts in shallow baking dish.
- **Cover**, and bake for 1 hour, or until chicken is no longer pink in the center and the juices run clear.

41. Spicy Turkey & Veggies

Servings: 5
Preparation time: 15 minutes
Cook time: 35 minutes
Ready in: 50 minutes

Nutrition Facts

Serving Size 316 g

Amount Per Serving

Calories 317	Calories from Fat 162

	% Daily Value*
Total Fat 18.0g	**28%**
Saturated Fat 3.9g	**20%**
Trans Fat 0.0g	
Cholesterol 93mg	**31%**
Sodium 293mg	**12%**
Total Carbohydrates 11.8g	**4%**
Dietary Fiber 3.3g	**13%**
Sugars 5.6g	
Protein 27.2g	

Vitamin A 88%	•	Vitamin C 66%
Calcium 6%	•	Iron 26%

Nutrition Grade B+

* Based on a 2000 calorie diet

Ingredients

- 2 tablespoons olive oil
- 4 cloves garlic, minced
- 1 large onion, chopped
- 1 pound ground turkey
- 1/2 teaspoon dried thyme leaves
- 1 teaspoon ground turmeric
- 1/2 teaspoon ground cayenne pepper
- 1 teaspoon ground cumin
- 1 pinch crushed red pepper flakes
- 1/2 teaspoon unrefined sea salt
- 1 cup zucchini, diced
- 1 cup carrots, diced
- 2 stalks celery, chopped
- 3 1/2 cups tomatoes, peeled, seeded, and chopped
- 1/2 cup organic low-sodium chicken broth

- 1/2 cup chopped parsley

Directions
- **Heat** olive oil in a large pot over medium-high heat.
- **Sauté** onion and garlic in olive oil for 2 minutes, or until onions are translucent.
- **Add** ground turkey and cook until no longer pink; season with thyme, turmeric, cayenne pepper, cumin, red pepper flakes, and salt.
- **Stir** in zucchini, carrots, celery, tomatoes, and chicken broth then reduce heat to low.
- **Simmer** for 25 minutes or until vegetables are tender. Stir in parsley and serve.

42. Coconut Chicken Curry

Servings: 7
Preparation time: 10 minutes
Cook time: 40 minutes
Ready in: 50 minutes

Nutrition Facts

Serving Size 299 g

Amount Per Serving

Calories 420   Calories from Fat 224

	% Daily Value*
Total Fat 24.9g	**38%**
Saturated Fat 15.2g	**76%**
Trans Fat 0.0g	
Cholesterol 87mg	**29%**
Sodium 543mg	**23%**
Total Carbohydrates 21.1g	**7%**
Dietary Fiber 4.3g	**17%**
Sugars 15.7g	
Protein 31.1g	

Vitamin A 62%	Vitamin C 19%
Calcium 6%	Iron 19%

Nutrition Grade B
* Based on a 2000 calorie diet

Ingredients
- 1 1/2 pounds boneless skinless pasture-fed, free-range chicken breasts, cut into 1/2-inch chunks

- 1 teaspoon unrefined sea salt
- 1 teaspoon ground black pepper
- 2 tablespoons curry powder
- 1 1/2 tablespoons olive oil
- 1/2 onion, thinly sliced
- 2 cloves garlic, crushed
- 1 cup carrots, diced
- 1/2 cup celery, chopped
- 1 3/4 cup pure coconut milk
- 1 3/4 cup can stewed, diced tomatoes
- 1 cup tomato sauce
- 3 tablespoons raw honey

Directions

- **Place** chicken chunks in a bowl and sprinkle with salt, pepper, and curry powder; toss to coat.
- **Heat** olive oil in a large skillet over medium-high heat.
- **Sauté** onions and garlic in olive oil for 1 minute. Reduce heat to medium.
- **Add** chicken and cook for 7 to 10 minutes, or until chicken is no longer pink in center and juices run clear. Add carrots and celery, simmer until tender.
- **Stir** in coconut milk, tomatoes, tomato sauce, and honey. Cover and simmer for 30 minutes; stirring occasionally.
- **Serve** warm.

43. Peach Pork Chops

Servings: 4
Preparation time: 10 minutes
Cook time: 25 minutes
Ready in: 35 minutes

Nutrition Facts

Serving Size 205 g

Amount Per Serving

Calories 241	Calories from Fat 73

	% Daily Value*
Total Fat 8.1g	**12%**
Saturated Fat 1.9g	**10%**
Trans Fat 0.0g	
Cholesterol 83mg	**28%**
Sodium 157mg	**7%**
Total Carbohydrates 11.2g	**4%**
Dietary Fiber 1.8g	**7%**
Sugars 8.7g	
Protein 30.9g	

Vitamin A 8%	•	Vitamin C 12%
Calcium 3%	•	Iron 12%

Nutrition Grade A
* Based on a 2000 calorie diet

Ingredients
- 2 fresh peaches, peeled, cored, and diced
- 1/4 cup water
- 1 tablespoons raw honey
- 2 tablespoons Dijon mustard
- 2 teaspoons curry powder
- 1/2 teaspoon ground cinnamon
- 1 teaspoon ground ginger
- 1 tablespoon olive oil
- 4 (1/4-pound) boneless pork chops
- 2 green onions, chopped
- 2 tablespoons chopped fresh parsley

Directions
- **Place** the peaches, water, and honey in a small saucepan over medium-high heat. Cook for 8 to minutes, or until tender.

120

- **Puree** the peach mixture in blender until smooth then pour into a bowl. Add mustard, curry powder, cinnamon, and ginger to the peach mixture.
- **Heat** the olive oil in a skillet over medium heat. Add the pork chops and cook for 8 minutes, or until cooked through.
- **Pour** the peach mixture over the pork chops; simmer until heated through.
- **Sprinkle** parsley over the top and serve.

44. Spicy Beef and Veggie Curry

Servings: 4
Preparation time: 15 minutes
Cook time: 43 minutes
Ready in: 1 hour 15 minutes

Nutrition Facts

Serving Size 216 g

Amount Per Serving

Calories 296   Calories from Fat 143

	% Daily Value*
Total Fat 15.9g	**24%**
Saturated Fat 7.7g	**39%**
Trans Fat 0.0g	
Cholesterol 87mg	**29%**
Sodium 472mg	**20%**
Total Carbohydrates 7.0g	**2%**
Dietary Fiber 2.4g	**10%**
Sugars 2.9g	
Protein 31.4g	

Vitamin A 70%	•	Vitamin C 26%
Calcium 4%	•	Iron 113%

Nutrition Grade A-

* Based on a 2000 calorie diet

Ingredients
- 2 tablespoons olive oil
- 2 cloves garlic, crushed
- 1 large onion, finely sliced
- 1/4 teaspoons red pepper flakes
- 3 Jalapeno peppers, thinly sliced

- 1 1/2 teaspoons ground cumin
- 1 teaspoon turmeric
- 1 teaspoon ground coriander
- 1/2 teaspoon ground cardamom
- 1/2 teaspoon chili powder
- 1/4 teaspoons ground black pepper
- 1/4 teaspoon ground cinnamon
- 1/4 teaspoon ground cloves
- 1 1/2 pounds beef sirloin, cubed
- 1 teaspoon unrefined sea salt
- 5 cups spinach
- 1/2 cup carrots, diced
- 1 cup tomatoes, chopped
- 2/3 cup pure coconut milk
- 1 teaspoon lemon juice

Directions

- **Heat** the olive oil in a large saucepan over medium heat. Add garlic and onion, and sauté for 5 minutes until softened.
- **Add** jalapeno peppers continue to cook for 3 minutes more.
- **Mix** cumin, turmeric, coriander, cardamom, chili powder, black pepper, cinnamon, and cloves in a small bowl.
- **Add** the beef and sprinkle with cumin mixture and salt, cook for 5 minutes more; stirring occasionally.
- **Stir** in the spinach, carrots, tomatoes, and coconut milk. Cover and simmer for 20 minutes, stirring occasionally.
- **Drizzle** with lemon juice, and cook for another 10 minutes, or until the sauce thickens.

45. Grilled Swordfish with Parsley Walnut Pesto

Servings: 4
Preparation time: 15 minutes
Cook time: 10 minutes
Ready in: 25 minutes

```
Nutrition Facts
Serving Size 163 g

Amount Per Serving
Calories 313          Calories from Fat 145
                            % Daily Value*
Total Fat 16.1g                          25%
  Saturated Fat 3.2g                     16%
  Trans Fat 0.0g
Cholesterol 73mg                         24%
Sodium 586mg                             24%
Total Carbohydrates 1.8g                  1%
  Dietary Fiber 0.7g                      3%
Protein 39.1g

Vitamin A 11%          •      Vitamin C 12%
Calcium 5%             •            Iron 11%

Nutrition Grade B
* Based on a 2000 calorie diet
```

Ingredients

- 4 (5 ounce) swordfish fillets
- 1/2 teaspoon unrefined sea salt
- 1/4 teaspoon ground black pepper
- 1/4 teaspoon red pepper flakes
  Parsley Walnut Pesto:
- 1/4 cup chopped walnuts
- 1 tablespoon grass-fed raw milk Parmesan cheese, grated (recommended: Organic Valley)
- 2 cloves garlic
- 1 tablespoon extra-virgin olive oil
- 1/4 cup packed fresh parsley leaves
- 1/2 teaspoon unrefined sea salt
- 1/8 teaspoon ground black pepper
  Note: For strict Paleo version, omit cheese

Directions

- **Preheat** grill for medium-high heat.
- **Rub** both sides of the fish fillets with salt, black pepper, and red pepper flakes.
- **Grill** fish for 4 minutes each side, or until golden and flaky. Place grilled swordfish on individual plates.
- **Combine** walnuts, cheese, and garlic in a blender or food processor and process until finely chopped. Drizzle with olive oil, parsley, salt and pepper then process until smooth.
- **Top** grilled swordfish with the parsley walnut pesto to serve.

46. Chili Turkey Stew

Servings: 4
Preparation time: 15 minutes
Cook time: 18 minutes
Ready in: 33 minutes

Nutrition Facts

Serving Size 394 g

Amount Per Serving

Calories 230	Calories from Fat 96

	% Daily Value*
Total Fat 10.6g	**16%**
Saturated Fat 1.5g	**7%**
Trans Fat 0.0g	
Cholesterol 47mg	**16%**
Sodium 491mg	**20%**
Total Carbohydrates 11.0g	**4%**
Dietary Fiber 2.1g	**9%**
Sugars 3.1g	
Protein 22.9g	

Vitamin A 33%	•	Vitamin C 19%
Calcium 3%	•	Iron 11%

Nutrition Grade C
* Based on a 2000 calorie diet

Ingredients
- 2 tablespoons olive oil
- 4 garlic cloves, minced
- 1 onion, diced
- 1/2 cup green chilies, diced
- 2 tablespoons ground coriander

- 1 tablespoon dried basil
- 1/4 teaspoon ground cayenne pepper
- 1/4 teaspoon ground black pepper
- 4 cups organic low-sodium vegetable broth
- 3 cups cooked lean turkey breast, chopped
- 1/4 cup fresh parsley, chopped

Directions

- **Heat** olive oil in a large soup pan over medium-high heat. Add garlic and onion, sauté until onions are translucent.
- **Stir** in the green chilies, coriander, basil, cayenne pepper, and black pepper.
- **Pour** in vegetable broth and bring to a boil. Reduce heat to medium low, and cook for 10 minutes.
- **Add** the turkey and cook stew for 5 minutes more. Sprinkle chopped parsley over the top and serve.

47. Sweet Potato Cottage Pie

Servings: 3
Preparation time: 10 minutes
Cook time: 45 minutes
Ready in: 55 minutes

Nutrition Facts

Serving Size 222 g

Amount Per Serving

Calories 258   Calories from Fat 86

	% Daily Value*
Total Fat 9.5g	**15%**
Saturated Fat 4.2g	**21%**
Trans Fat 0.0g	
Cholesterol 68mg	**23%**
Sodium 371mg	**15%**
Total Carbohydrates 17.2g	**6%**
Dietary Fiber 3.3g	**13%**
Sugars 6.6g	
Protein 26.0g	

Vitamin A 234%	•	Vitamin C 28%
Calcium 4%	•	Iron 88%

Nutrition Grade A

* Based on a 2000 calorie diet

Ingredients

- 1 large sweet potato
- 1 tablespoon grass-fed raw milk butter (recommended: Organic Valley)
- 1 tablespoon pure coconut milk
- 1/8 teaspoon unrefined sea salt
- 1/8 teaspoon ground black pepper
- 1 teaspoon olive oil
- 1 clove garlic, crushed and chopped
- 1/4 cup onion, chopped
- 1/2 pound lean ground beef
- 1 cup mushrooms, diced
- 1/2 cup tomato sauce
- 1/4 teaspoon ground cinnamon
- 1/4 teaspoon ground nutmeg
- 1/4 teaspoon dried rosemary

Directions

- **Scrub** the sweet potatoes clean then pierce the skin with a fork. Place sweet potatoes on a microwave-safe dish. Set the microwave on high, and cook for 10-12 minutes or until tender, turning once.
- **Cool** and cut in half; scoop out the pulp and place in a small bowl. Mash with butter, milk, salt and pepper; set aside.
- **Preheat** oven to 350°f. Grease a baking dish with olive oil.
- **Heat** olive oil in a large skillet over medium heat. Sauté garlic and onion in olive oil, cook until onion is translucent and garlic is lightly browned.
- **Add** the ground beef and cook until meat is no longer pink; drain. Stir in mushrooms, tomato sauce, cinnamon, nutmeg, and rosemary. Pour mixture onto the baking dish.
- **Spread** mashed sweet potato evenly over meat mixture.
- **Bake** for 25-30 minutes.

48. Cranberry Spinach Salad

Servings: 8
Ready in: 15 minutes

Nutrition Facts

Serving Size 164 g

Amount Per Serving

Calories 362	Calories from Fat 251

% Daily Value*

Total Fat 27.9g	**43%**
Saturated Fat 3.4g	**17%**
Trans Fat 0.0g	
Cholesterol 0mg	**0%**
Sodium 127mg	**5%**
Total Carbohydrates 28.2g	**9%**
Dietary Fiber 4.4g	**17%**
Sugars 18.9g	
Protein 5.6g	

Vitamin A 64%	•	Vitamin C 44%
Calcium 10%	•	Iron 11%

Nutrition Grade B

* Based on a 2000 calorie diet

Ingredients

- 8 cups baby spinach leaves
- 1 1/2 cup mandarin oranges, drained
- 1 cup raisins
- 1 cup green apple, cubed
- 1/2 medium red onion, sliced into rings
- 1 1/2 cups roasted almonds, sliced
- 1/4 cup cider vinegar
- 2 teaspoons raw honey
- 3 cloves garlic, chopped
- 1/2 teaspoon unrefined sea salt
- 1/2 teaspoon freshly ground black pepper
- 3/4 cup olive oil

Directions

- **Place** spinach onto salad plates. Arrange the oranges, raisins, apple, onions, and almonds on top.

- **Whisk** together the vinegar, honey, garlic, salt, and pepper. Whisk in olive oil by droplets.
- **Drizzle** dressing over salad.

49. Pork Carnitas

Servings: 4
Preparation time: 10 minutes
Cook time: 2 hours
Ready in: 2 hours 10 minutes

Nutrition Facts

Serving Size 233 g

Amount Per Serving

Calories 209 — Calories from Fat 38

	% Daily Value*
Total Fat 4.2g	**6%**
Saturated Fat 1.4g	**7%**
Trans Fat 0.0g	
Cholesterol 83mg	**28%**
Sodium 471mg	**20%**
Total Carbohydrates 11.0g	**4%**
Dietary Fiber 2.6g	**11%**
Sugars 6.8g	
Protein 30.8g	

Vitamin A 55%	•	Vitamin C 56%
Calcium 4%	•	Iron 11%

Nutrition Grade A

* Based on a 2000 calorie diet

Ingredients

- 1 pound boneless pork shoulder
- 1 clove garlic, crushed
- 1 onion, cut into 4 wedges
- 1 carrot, peeled and cut into 1 inch pieces
- 1 jalapeno, seeded and ribs removed, chopped
- 1 stalk celery, cut into 1 inch pieces
- 1 tomato, chopped
- 1 orange, juiced
- 1 teaspoon unrefined sea salt
- 1/4 teaspoon ground coriander
- 1/4 teaspoon dried thyme
- 1/4 teaspoon ground black pepper
- 1/4 teaspoon ground cayenne pepper
- 1 bay leaf

Directions

- **Place** the pork in a saucepan then top with garlic, onion, carrot, jalapeno, celery, and tomato. Drizzle with orange juice.
- **Season** with salt, coriander, thyme, pepper, cayenne, and bay leaf then cover with enough water.
- **Bring** to a boil over medium heat. Reduce heat to low and simmer covered for 2 hours until pork is tender. Cool and shred.

50. Broiled Herbed Halibut

Servings: 4
Preparation time: 10 minutes
Cook time: 15-20 minutes
Ready in: 25 minutes

Nutrition Facts

Serving Size 130 g

Amount Per Serving

Calories 195   Calories from Fat 62

	% Daily Value*
Total Fat 6.9g	**11%**
Saturated Fat 1.0g	**5%**
Cholesterol 46mg	**15%**
Sodium 275mg	**11%**
Total Carbohydrates 1.5g	**0%**
Dietary Fiber 0.5g	**2%**
Protein 30.5g	

Vitamin A 5%	•	Vitamin C 8%
Calcium 8%	•	Iron 8%

Nutrition Grade B+

* Based on a 2000 calorie diet

Ingredients

- 1 (2 pound) halibut fillet, rinsed and patted dry
- 2 tablespoons olive oil
- 1 large lemon, juiced
- 1 teaspoon unrefined sea salt
- 1/2 teaspoon ground black pepper
- 2 cloves garlic, crushed and chopped
- 1 tablespoon basil leaves, chopped

- 2 teaspoons ground fennel seeds
- 1/4 cup fennel leaves, roughly chopped
- olive oil for greasing

Directions
- **Grease** a baking sheet with olive oil.
- **Place** halibut on the baking sheet, and coat with 2 tablespoons olive oil.
- **Drizzle** entire fillet with lemon juice then season with salt, pepper, garlic, basil, and fennel seeds.
- **Broil** halibut in the oven for 15 to 20 minutes or until opaque and easily flakes with a fork.
- **Sprinkle** fennel leaves over the top and serve.

51. Crock Pot Apple Pork Roast

Servings: 6
Preparation time: 10 minutes
Cook time: 6 hours
Ready in: 6 hours 10 minutes

Nutrition Facts

Serving Size 255 g

Amount Per Serving

Calories 329   Calories from Fat 101

% Daily Value*

Total Fat 11.3g	**17%**
Saturated Fat 3.9g	**20%**
Trans Fat 0.0g	
Cholesterol 98mg	**33%**
Sodium 194mg	**8%**
Total Carbohydrates 23.4g	**8%**
Dietary Fiber 4.7g	**19%**
Sugars 16.1g	
Protein 33.1g	

Vitamin A 2%	•	Vitamin C 14%
Calcium 6%	•	Iron 11%

Nutrition Grade B+

* Based on a 2000 calorie diet

Ingredients
- 1 (1.5 pound) pork roast

- 4 apples, sliced and cored
- 1 clove garlic, minced
- 1 small white onion, sliced
- 2 tablespoons ground cinnamon
- 1 tablespoon mustard
- 1 tablespoon dried basil
- 1 tablespoon raw honey
- 1/2 teaspoon unrefined sea salt
- 1/4 teaspoon ground black pepper

Directions
- **Place** all ingredients into the crock pot and pour 1 cup of water.
- **Cook** on low for 6 hours.
- **Shred** pork using two forks or tongs. Serve hot.

52. Zucchini and Carrot Meatballs

Servings: 4
Preparation time: 20 minutes
Cook time: 28 minutes
Ready in: 48 minutes

Nutrition Facts

Serving Size 241 g

Amount Per Serving

Calories 385   Calories from Fat 217

	% Daily Value*
Total Fat 24.2g	**37%**
Saturated Fat 6.6g	**33%**
Trans Fat 0.0g	
Cholesterol 157mg	**52%**
Sodium 528mg	**22%**
Total Carbohydrates 7.3g	**2%**
Dietary Fiber 6.0g	**24%**
Sugars 2.9g	
Protein 30.3g	

Vitamin A 124%	•	Vitamin C 15%
Calcium 9%	•	Iron 25%

Nutrition Grade B
* Based on a 2000 calorie diet

Ingredients

- 2 tablespoons olive oil
- 2 cloves garlic, minced
- 1 small zucchini, diced
- 2 large carrots, diced
- 1 pound grass-fed lean ground beef
- 3/4 teaspoon ground black pepper
- 2 eggs
- 1/2 cup almond flour
- 1/4 cup flaxseed meal
- 1 teaspoon unrefined sea salt
- 1/2 teaspoon black pepper
- 1/2 teaspoon fresh cilantro, chopped
- 1/2 teaspoon thyme, chopped
- 1 teaspoon dried oregano
- 1/4 cup onion, chopped

Directions

- **Heat** olive oil in a medium skillet over medium heat. Add garlic and sauté until lightly browned. Add zucchini and carrots, cook until soft, about 3 to 5 minutes; set aside.
- **Combine** the ground beef and remaining ingredients in a large bowl.
- **Shape** mixture into meatballs and place on a baking sheet
- **Bake** at 350 degrees f for 25-30 minutes. Serve warm.

53. Chicken Cacciatore with Mushrooms

Servings: 4
Preparation time: 10 minutes
Cook time: 12 minutes
Ready in: 22 minutes

```
Nutrition Facts
Serving Size 142 g

Amount Per Serving
Calories 264          Calories from Fat 152
                              % Daily Value*
Total Fat 16.9g                        26%
  Saturated Fat 3.2g                   16%
Cholesterol 76mg                       25%
Sodium 75mg                             3%
Total Carbohydrates 2.6g                1%
  Dietary Fiber 0.7g                    3%
  Sugars 1.3g
Protein 25.3g

Vitamin A 6%          •          Vitamin C 25%
Calcium 2%            •                Iron 9%
Nutrition Grade B-
* Based on a 2000 calorie diet
```

Ingredients

- 3 tablespoons olive oil
- 1/3 cup chopped onion
- 1 clove garlic, chopped
- 1/3 cup green bell pepper, chopped
- 3/4 pound pasture-fed, free-range chicken meat, cooked and cubed
- 1/2 cup mushrooms, sliced
- 1/2 cup whole tomatoes, peeled
- 1/4 teaspoon dried thyme

Directions

- **Heat** olive oil a large skillet over medium-high heat. Add garlic, bell pepper, and onion and sauté until soft, about 3 to 5 minutes.
- **Stir** in chicken, mushrooms, tomatoes, and thyme. Reduce heat to medium low.

- **Simmer** for 8 to 10 minutes, stirring frequently.
- **Serve** hot.

54. Herb Crusted Chicken

Servings: 6
Preparation time: 15 minutes
Cook time: 25 minutes
Ready in: 40 minutes

Nutrition Facts

Serving Size 160 g

Amount Per Serving

Calories 243	Calories from Fat 112

	% Daily Value*
Total Fat 12.4g	**19%**
Saturated Fat 3.4g	**17%**
Trans Fat 0.0g	
Cholesterol 71mg	**24%**
Sodium 126mg	**5%**
Total Carbohydrates 0.3g	**0%**
Dietary Fiber 3.0g	**12%**
Protein 29.4g	

Vitamin A 2%	•	Vitamin C 0%
Calcium 9%	•	Iron 8%

Nutrition Grade B+
* Based on a 2000 calorie diet

Ingredients

- 3 pasture-fed, free-range eggs
- 3/4 cup almond flour
- 1/4 cup flaxseed meal
- 1 tablespoon flax seeds
- 1/2 teaspoon dried thyme
- 1/2 teaspoon dried basil
- 1 clove garlic, finely chopped
- 1/4 cup grated grass-fed raw milk Parmesan cheese (recommended: Organic Valley)
- 1/2 teaspoon unrefined sea salt
- 1/4 teaspoon freshly ground black pepper
- 1 pound boneless, skinless pasture-fed, free-range chicken breasts, pound flat and cut into long strips, 1-inch wide
  Note: For strict Paleo version, omit cheese

Directions

- **Preheat** oven to 350° f.
- **Beat** eggs in a shallow bowl.
- **Mix** almond flour, flaxseed meal, flax seeds, thyme, basil, garlic, cheese, salt, and pepper in a plate.
- **Dip** chicken in egg then dredge both sides evenly in the almond flour mixture. Place chicken on a baking sheet.
- **Bake** for about 25-35 minutes, or until fully cooked.

55. Cauliflower Rice

Serving: 1
Preparation time: 10 minutes
Cook time: 10 minutes
Ready in: 10 minutes

Nutrition Facts

Serving Size 280 g

Amount Per Serving

Calories 66	Calories from Fat 2

	% Daily Value*
Total Fat 0.3g	0%
Cholesterol 0mg	0%
Sodium 80mg	3%
Total Carbohydrates 14.1g	5%
Dietary Fiber 6.6g	27%
Sugars 6.4g	
Protein 5.2g	

Vitamin A 1%	•	Vitamin C 205%
Calcium 6%	•	Iron 7%

Nutrition Grade A
* Based on a 2000 calorie diet

Ingredients

- 1 head organic cauliflower
- 1 tablespoon water

Directions

- **Wash**, and remove core and leaves of cauliflower.
- **Place** florets in a bowl of food processor and process until evenly chopped but not completely pulverized.

- **Place** cauliflower rice and water in a microwave-safe covered dish.
- **Cook** cauliflower in microwave on high until tender, about 7 minutes.

PALEO DESSERT and SNACK

56. Coconut Ice Cream with Walnuts and Dark Chocolate

Servings: 8
Ready in: 40 minutes

Nutrition Facts

Serving Size 108 g

Amount Per Serving	
Calories 332	Calories from Fat 228
	% Daily Value*
Total Fat 25.3g	**39%**
Saturated Fat 17.3g	**87%**
Cholesterol 0mg	**0%**
Sodium 12mg	**0%**
Total Carbohydrates 28.9g	**10%**
Dietary Fiber 3.2g	**13%**
Sugars 24.4g	
Protein 3.7g	

Vitamin A 0%	Vitamin C 5%
Calcium 2%	Iron 17%

Nutrition Grade C+
* Based on a 2000 calorie diet

Ingredients

- 2 cups pure coconut milk, chilled
- 1/2 cup raw honey
- 1 cup chopped hazelnuts
- 1 cup coconut flakes
- 1/2 cup dark chocolate chips (70%-90% cocoa)

Directions

- **Place** chopped walnuts in a small skillet over medium-low heat. Cook for 3 minutes, stirring frequently until lightly browned. Cool and set aside.
- **Stir** together coconut milk and honey. Freeze about 20-30 minutes, or according to ice cream maker instructions.
- **Add** toasted hazelnuts, coconut flakes, and chocolate chips to the ice cream maker during the last 5 minutes of freezing.

57. Fresh Pumpkin Squares

Servings: 7
Preparation time: 10 minutes
Cook time: 40 minutes
Ready in: 50 minutes

Nutrition Facts

Serving Size 219 g

Amount Per Serving

Calories 270	Calories from Fat 133

	% Daily Value*
Total Fat 14.8g	**23%**
Saturated Fat 8.1g	**40%**
Cholesterol 94mg	**31%**
Sodium 430mg	**18%**
Total Carbohydrates 33.0g	**11%**
Dietary Fiber 4.8g	**19%**
Sugars 24.7g	
Protein 6.4g	

Vitamin A 406%	•	Vitamin C 11%
Calcium 7%	•	Iron 16%

Nutrition Grade B
* Based on a 2000 calorie diet

Ingredients

- 1 (2 pounds) fresh pie pumpkin
- 4 eggs
- 1/2 cup raw honey
- 1/4 cup coconut oil
- 2 cups almond flour
- 3 1/2 teaspoons pumpkin pie spice
- 1 teaspoon baking soda

- 1/2 teaspoon baking soda mixed with 3 teaspoons lemon juice
- 1/2 teaspoon unrefined sea salt

Directions
- **Cut** the pumpkin in half and scrape out the seeds using a melon baller.
- **Pour** a couple of inches of water in a large pot over medium heat. Place the pumpkin in a steamer basket.
- **Cover** and steam the pumpkin for 15 to 20 minutes until soft. Let cool then scoop out the cooked pumpkin from the peel. Place in a blender and puree until smooth.
- **Preheat** oven to 350 degrees f. Grease a 9x13 inch baking pan with coconut oil.
- **Whisk** together the eggs, honey, coconut oil, and pumpkin puree until smooth.
- **Sift** together the flour, pumpkin pie spice, baking soda, baking soda-lemon juice mixture, and salt then stir into the pumpkin mixture. Spread batter into the baking pan.
- **Bake** for 25 to 30 minutes. Cool, cut into squares, and serve.

58. Banana Bread with Almonds

Servings: 12
Preparation time: 15 minutes
Cook time: 1 hour
Ready in: 1 hour 15 minutes

Nutrition Facts

Serving Size 112 g

Amount Per Serving

Calories 210   Calories from Fat 75

	% Daily Value*
Total Fat 8.3g	**13%**
Saturated Fat 0.8g	**4%**
Trans Fat 0.0g	
Cholesterol 33mg	**11%**
Sodium 181mg	**8%**
Total Carbohydrates 33.6g	**11%**
Dietary Fiber 3.0g	**12%**
Sugars 27.0g	
Protein 4.6g	

Vitamin A 1%	•	Vitamin C 6%
Calcium 5%	•	Iron 6%

Nutrition Grade B

* Based on a 2000 calorie diet

Ingredients

- Coconut oil for greasing
- 1/2 cup organic applesauce
- 3/4 cup raw honey
- 1 teaspoon ground cinnamon
- 2 eggs, beaten
- 2 1/3 cups mashed overripe bananas
- 2 cups almond flour
- 1 teaspoon baking soda
- 1/4 teaspoon unrefined sea salt
- 3/4 cup almond nuts, chopped

Directions

- **Preheat** oven to 350 degrees F. Lightly grease a 9x5 inch loaf pan with coconut oil.
- **Whisk** together applesauce, honey, and cinnamon in a medium bowl. Stir in eggs and mashed bananas until well blended.
- **Combine** the almond flour, baking soda, and salt in another bowl. Pour banana mixture into flour mixture then fold in chopped almonds; stir until well blended. Pour batter into the loaf pan.

- **Bake** for 1 hour, or until a toothpick inserted into center of the loaf comes out clean.
- **Let** cool, slice, and serve.

59. Berries and Coconut Cream Parfaits

Servings: 5
Ready in: 10 minutes

Nutrition Facts

Serving Size 138 g

Amount Per Serving

Calories 322	Calories from Fat 230

	% Daily Value*
Total Fat 25.5g	**39%**
Saturated Fat 10.8g	**54%**
Trans Fat 0.0g	
Cholesterol 0mg	**0%**
Sodium 17mg	**1%**
Total Carbohydrates 20.1g	**7%**
Dietary Fiber 4.6g	**18%**
Sugars 12.7g	
Protein 7.6g	

Vitamin A 2%	•	Vitamin C 16%
Calcium 3%	•	Iron 10%

Nutrition Grade C+
* Based on a 2000 calorie diet

Ingredients
- 1 cup fresh blueberries
- 1 cup fresh raspberries
- 1 cup organic coconut cream
- 1 cup walnuts, chopped
- 1 tablespoon fresh mint leaves, chopped
- 2 tablespoons raw honey

Directions
- **Combine** berries in a bowl then divide evenly among parfait glasses.
- **Stir** together the coconut cream and honey then pour over berries.
- **Sprinkle** chopped walnuts and mint over the top.

- **Chill** and serve.

60. Ginger Brownies

Servings: 8
Preparation time: 10 minuets
Cook time: 35 minutes
Total time: 45 minutes

Nutrition Facts

Serving Size 90 g

Amount Per Serving

Calories 305	Calories from Fat 159

	% Daily Value*
Total Fat 17.7g	**27%**
Saturated Fat 12.2g	**61%**
Trans Fat 0.0g	
Cholesterol 126mg	**42%**
Sodium 73mg	**3%**
Total Carbohydrates 32.8g	**11%**
Dietary Fiber 4.7g	**19%**
Sugars 24.8g	
Protein 7.2g	

Vitamin A 4%	•	Vitamin C 0%
Calcium 5%	•	Iron 11%

Nutrition Grade D+

* Based on a 2000 calorie diet

Ingredients
- 1/3 cup coconut oil, melted
- 1/2 cup cocoa, sifted
- 6 eggs
- 1/2 cup raw honey
- 1 teaspoon pure vanilla extract
- 100g dark chocolate (70%-90% cocoa), chopped
- 1/2 cup coconut flour
- 1 teaspoon freshly grated nutmeg
- 1 tablespoon fresh ginger, minced
- Coconut oil for greasing

Directions
- **Preheat** oven to 356°f. Lightly grease a 9x9 inch baking pan with coconut oil.

- **Place** a medium saucepan over low heat. Heat the coconut oil and cocoa in the pan; stir to combine. Remove from heat and set aside.
- **Whisk** together the eggs, honey and vanilla in a bowl. Add the cocoa mixture, dark chocolate, coconut flour, ginger, and nutmeg; blend well.
- **Bake** for 30 to 35 minutes, or until a toothpick inserted into center comes out clean or with only a few crumbs sticking to it.
- **Cool**, slice into squares, and serve.

61. Minty Chocolate Cookies

Servings: 3
Preparation time: 20 minutes
Cook time: 10 minutes
Ready in: 30 minutes

Nutrition Facts

Serving Size 95 g

Amount Per Serving

Calories 308   Calories from Fat 212

	% Daily Value*
Total Fat 23.6g	**36%**
Saturated Fat 16.1g	**80%**
Cholesterol 3mg	**1%**
Sodium 90mg	**4%**
Total Carbohydrates 22.8g	**8%**
Dietary Fiber 1.6g	**6%**
Sugars 19.4g	
Protein 3.5g	

Vitamin A 1%	•	Vitamin C 0%
Calcium 5%	•	Iron 5%

Nutrition Grade F
* Based on a 2000 calorie diet

Ingredients
- 1 cup almond flour
- 1/8 teaspoon unrefined sea salt
- 1/8 teaspoon baking soda
- 1/4 cup dark chocolate, chopped (70%-90% cocoa)
- 3 tablespoons coconut oil, melted
- 2 tablespoons raw honey
- 1 tablespoon pure coconut milk

- 1 tablespoon pure mint extract
- 1 teaspoon almond extract

Directions
- **Preheat** oven to 350 degrees f. Line a baking sheet with parchment paper.
- **Combine** the almond flour, salt, baking soda, and dark chocolate in a medium bowl. Whisk together coconut oil, honey, coconut milk, mint extract, and almond extract in a small bowl. Pour wet mixture over dry mixture.
- **Fill** a tablespoon or cookie scoop with batter. Scoop out batter (about 2 tablespoons per cookie) and drop 2 inches apart out onto prepared baking sheet and lightly press down in the center.
- **Bake** for 10-11 minutes, or until set. Cool and store cookies in a tightly covered cookie jar.

62. No-Bake Raisin Chocolate Truffles

Servings: 7
Ready in: 30 minutes

Nutrition Facts

Serving Size 103 g

Amount Per Serving

Calories 321   Calories from Fat 154

	% Daily Value*
Total Fat 17.1g	**26%**
Saturated Fat 1.2g	**6%**
Trans Fat 0.0g	
Cholesterol 0mg	**0%**
Sodium 14mg	**1%**
Total Carbohydrates 36.1g	**12%**
Dietary Fiber 7.8g	**31%**
Sugars 18.1g	
Protein 9.2g	

Vitamin A 4%	•	Vitamin C 1%	
Calcium 2%	•	Iron 14%	

Nutrition Grade D+

* Based on a 2000 calorie diet

Ingredients
- 2 cups almond flour
- 1/4 cup flax meal

- 1 cup dried prunes
- 1 tablespoon pure vanilla extract
- 1 tablespoon raw honey
- 1/4 cup water
- 1/2 cup raisins
- 1/4 cup natural Cocoa Powder

Directions
- **Combine** almond flour and flax meal in a bowl. Add vanilla, honey, and water, stir until smooth.
- **Place** dried prunes in a food processor or blender and process until finely chopped. Stir the chopped prunes and raisins into the flour mixture. Refrigerate mixture for 10 minutes.
- **Shape** mixture into 1-inch balls then roll in cocoa powder until evenly coated.
- **Chill** covered for 10 minutes before serving.

63. Chocolate Banana Ice Cream with Hazelnuts

Servings: 8
Ready in: 1 hour and 10 minutes

Nutrition Facts
Serving Size 144 g

Amount Per Serving

Calories 219	Calories from Fat 92

	% Daily Value*
Total Fat 10.2g	**16%**
Saturated Fat 2.6g	**13%**
Trans Fat 0.0g	
Cholesterol 0mg	**0%**
Sodium 5mg	**0%**
Total Carbohydrates 32.6g	**11%**
Dietary Fiber 3.0g	**12%**
Sugars 20.1g	
Protein 4.0g	

Vitamin A 2%	•	Vitamin C 13%
Calcium 9%	•	Iron 6%

Nutrition Grade B+

* Based on a 2000 calorie diet

Ingredients
- 6 ripe bananas, peeled, sliced then frozen

- 1 cup pure coconut milk
- 1/4 cup almond butter
- 2 tablespoon raw honey
- 1/2 cup grated dark chocolate chips (70%-90% cocoa)
- 1/2 cup sliced hazelnuts

Directions
- **Place** bananas in food processor or blender and puree for 15 seconds. Stir in coconut milk, almond butter, honey, and chocolate chips; blend until smooth. Fold in hazelnuts.
- **Pour** mixture into a freezable container
- **Freeze** for 1 hour and serve.

64. Blueberry Peach Pie

Servings: 8
Preparation time: 10 minutes
Cook time: 45 minutes
Ready in: 55 minutes

Nutrition Facts

Serving Size 186 g

Amount Per Serving

Calories 306　　　　Calories from Fat 165

	% Daily Value*
Total Fat 18.3g	**28%**
Saturated Fat 2.7g	**13%**
Trans Fat 0.0g	
Cholesterol 0mg	**0%**
Sodium 48mg	**2%**
Total Carbohydrates 35.7g	**12%**
Dietary Fiber 4.3g	**17%**
Sugars 27.6g	
Protein 5.0g	

Vitamin A 6%	•	Vitamin C 13%	
Calcium 7%	•	Iron 7%	

Nutrition Grade C-

* Based on a 2000 calorie diet

Ingredients
- 4 cups fresh peaches, peeled, cored, and sliced
- 1 cup blueberries
- 1 cup chopped pecans
- 3 tablespoons almond flour

- 1/2 cup raw honey
- 1 teaspoon pure vanilla extract
- 1 teaspoon ground cinnamon
- 9-inch gluten-free double-crusts pie (recommended: Pillsbury)
- 2 tablespoons grass-fed raw milk butter, softened and cut into pieces (recommended: Organic Valley)

Directions
- **Preheat** oven to 400 degrees f
- **Place** peaches, blueberries, and pecans in a large bowl.
- **Combine** almond flour, honey, vanilla, and cinnamon then toss together with the fruit mixture.
- **Line** a 9-inch pie plate with bottom pie crust. Add fruit mixture and dot with butter. Roll out remaining crust on top and seal edges.
- **Bake** for 45 minutes.

65. Fresh Fruit Salad with Lemon Coconut Cream

Servings: 4
Ready in: 20 minutes

Nutrition Facts

Serving Size 245 g

Amount Per Serving

Calories 304	Calories from Fat 197

	% Daily Value*
Total Fat 21.9g	34%
Saturated Fat 13.2g	66%
Trans Fat 0.0g	
Cholesterol 0mg	0%
Sodium 12mg	0%
Total Carbohydrates 25.5g	9%
Dietary Fiber 6.9g	28%
Sugars 16.6g	
Protein 4.9g	

Vitamin A 3%	•	Vitamin C 60%
Calcium 6%	•	Iron 11%

Nutrition Grade B-
* Based on a 2000 calorie diet

Ingredients
- 1 red apple, cored and chopped
- 1 green apple, cored and chopped

- 1 peach, pitted and sliced
- 1 cup strawberries, hulled and sliced
- 1/2 cup dried cranberries
- 1/2 cup almond nuts, chopped
- 2 tablespoons freshly squeezed lemon juice
- 1 cup coconut cream

Directions
- **Combine** apples, peach, strawberries, dried cranberries, and almonds in a large salad bowl.
- **Stir** together lemon juice and coconut cream then pour over salad.
- **Chill** and serve.

66. Vanilla Crepes with Strawberries and Cashews

Servings: 6
Preparation time: 10 minutes
Cook time: 15 minutes
Ready in: 25 minutes

Nutrition Facts

Serving Size 239 g

Amount Per Serving

Calories 220	Calories from Fat 80

	% Daily Value*
Total Fat 8.9g	**14%**
Saturated Fat 3.1g	**16%**
Trans Fat 0.0g	
Cholesterol 105mg	**35%**
Sodium 145mg	**6%**
Total Carbohydrates 30.9g	**10%**
Dietary Fiber 0.7g	**3%**
Sugars 24.7g	
Protein 3.5g	

Vitamin A 5%	•	Vitamin C 13%
Calcium 15%	•	Iron 8%

Nutrition Grade C
* Based on a 2000 calorie diet

Ingredients
- 1 1/2 cups almond flour
- 1/2 teaspoon unrefined sea salt
- 3 egg yolks

- 1 1/2 cups pure coconut milk
- 2 tablespoons pure vanilla extract
- 1 teaspoon ground cinnamon
- 2 tablespoons raw honey
- 5 tablespoons grass-fed raw milk butter, melted (recommended: Organic Valley)
- 1/2 cup strawberries, sliced
- 1/2 cup cashews, halves
- 1/2 cup pure maple syrup
- Coconut oil for greasing

Directions
- **Combine** almond flour and salt in a large bowl. Whisk in the egg yolks, coconut milk, vanilla, cinnamon, honey, and butter.
- **Grease** a crepe pan with coconut oil then place over medium heat.
- **Pour** batter (about 1/4 cup for each crepe) into the pan and tip to thinly spread batter; brown on both sides.
- **Fill** crepes with strawberries, cashews, and maple syrup.

67. Blueberry Cheesecake Squares

Servings: 5
Preparation time: 10 minutes
Cook time: 32 minutes
Ready in: 42 minutes

Nutrition Facts

Serving Size 108 g

Amount Per Serving

Calories 324	Calories from Fat 188
	% Daily Value*
Total Fat 20.8g	**32%**
Saturated Fat 5.5g	**28%**
Trans Fat 0.0g	
Cholesterol 49mg	**16%**
Sodium 130mg	**5%**
Total Carbohydrates 30.8g	**10%**
Dietary Fiber 1.9g	**7%**
Sugars 24.2g	
Protein 7.3g	

Vitamin A 7%	•	Vitamin C 1%
Calcium 9%	•	Iron 7%

Nutrition Grade D
* Based on a 2000 calorie diet

Ingredients
- 1/4 cup almond butter, softened
- 1/4 cup raw honey
- 1/4 cup pecans, chopped
- 1 cup almond flour
- 1/4 cup pure blueberry jam
- 1/2 cup organic cream cheese, softened (recommended: Organic Valley)
- 2 tablespoons pure coconut milk
- 1 egg
- 1/2 teaspoon ground cinnamon
- 1/2 teaspoon pure vanilla extract

Directions
- **Preheat** oven to 350 degrees f.
- **Stir** together the butter, honey, flour, and pecans until crumbly.

152

- **Press** mixture into an 8-inch square baking pan.
- **Bake** for 12 to 15 minutes. Cool crust on wire rack.
- **Whisk** together the blueberry jam, cream cheese, egg, coconut milk, cinnamon, and vanilla. Spread filling mixture over baked crust.
- **Return** pan in the oven and bake for about 20 minutes. Let cool, cover, and chill. Cut into squares and serve.

Note: This recipe is not for strict Paleo diet

68. Raspberry Cupcakes with Pecans

Servings: 6
Preparation time: 15 minutes
Cook time: 20-25 minutes
Ready in: 35 minutes

Nutrition Facts

Serving Size 121 g

Amount Per Serving

Calories 283	Calories from Fat 131

	% Daily Value*
Total Fat 14.5g	**22%**
Saturated Fat 4.3g	**21%**
Cholesterol 149mg	**50%**
Sodium 263mg	**11%**
Total Carbohydrates 34.2g	**11%**
Dietary Fiber 2.7g	**11%**
Sugars 30.0g	
Protein 6.6g	

Vitamin A 4%	•	Vitamin C 7%
Calcium 3%	•	Iron 13%

Nutrition Grade C-

* Based on a 2000 calorie diet

Ingredients
- 1/2 cup coconut flour
- 1/2 cup coconut flakes
- 1 tablespoon pure cornstarch
- 1/2 teaspoon baking soda
- 1/4 teaspoon unrefined sea salt
- 4 large eggs
- 1/2 cup raw honey
- 1 tablespoon pure vanilla extract
- 1 teaspoon lemon zest, finely chopped

- 1/2 cup fresh raspberries, mashed
- 1/2 cup pecans, chopped

Directions
- **Preheat** oven to 350 degrees f. Line a 6-cup muffin tin with paper liners.
- **Mix** coconut flour, coconut flakes, cornstarch, baking soda, and salt in a medium bowl.
- **Whisk** together the eggs, honey, and vanilla extract in a large bowl.
- **Add** the dry ingredients to the wet ingredients and blend using a handheld mixer. Stir in the mashed raspberries, lemon zest, and chopped walnuts.
- **Divide** and scoop ¼ cup of batter into each muffin cup.
- **Bake** for 20-25 minutes. Let cool and serve.

69. Cherry Crisp with Walnut Topping

Servings: 14
Preparation time: 10 minutes
Cook time: 30-35 minutes
Ready in: 40 minutes

Nutrition Facts
Serving Size 115 g

Amount Per Serving

Calories 224   Calories from Fat 80

	% Daily Value*
Total Fat 8.9g	**14%**
Saturated Fat 2.3g	**12%**
Trans Fat 0.0g	
Cholesterol 0mg	**0%**
Sodium 63mg	**3%**
Total Carbohydrates 34.6g	**12%**
Dietary Fiber 1.7g	**7%**
Sugars 10.1g	
Protein 3.3g	

Vitamin A 3%	•	Vitamin C 5%	
Calcium 2%	•	Iron 3%	

Nutrition Grade D
* Based on a 2000 calorie diet

Ingredients
- 1 cup chopped walnuts

- 3/4 cups almond flour, divided
- 1/2 cup unsweetened coconut flakes
- 1/2 cup raw honey, divided
- 1/4 teaspoon unrefined sea salt
- 1 teaspoon pure vanilla extract
- 1/3 cup grass-fed raw milk butter, melted (recommended: Organic Valley)
- 4 cups fresh cherries
- 1 teaspoon ground cinnamon
- Coconut oil for greasing

Directions

- **Preheat** oven to 350 degrees f (175 degrees c). Grease an 8x8 inch baking pan with coconut oil.
- **Toss** together the walnuts, 1/2 cup almond flour, coconut flakes, 1/4 cup honey, salt, and vanilla, and butter in a large bowl until crumbly.
- **Mix** the cherries, 1/4 cup honey, 1/4 cup almond flour, and cinnamon in the baking pan. Spoon the prepared crumble topping over the top.
- **Bake** for about 30-35 minutes.

70. Coconut Vanilla Ice cream with Balsamic Strawberries

Servings: 8
Preparation time: 15 minutes
Cook time: 8 minutes
Ready in: 23 minutes

Nutrition Facts

Serving Size 132 g

Amount Per Serving

Calories 261	Calories from Fat 137

	% Daily Value*
Total Fat 15.2g	**23%**
Saturated Fat 12.8g	**64%**
Trans Fat 0.0g	
Cholesterol 0mg	**0%**
Sodium 10mg	**0%**
Total Carbohydrates 32.6g	**11%**
Dietary Fiber 1.9g	**8%**
Sugars 30.2g	
Protein 2.0g	

Vitamin A 0%	•	Vitamin C 42%
Calcium 2%	•	Iron 7%

Nutrition Grade D+
* Based on a 2000 calorie diet

Ingredients
Coconut Vanilla Ice Cream:
- 2 cups ice cold pure full-fat coconut milk
- 1/2 cup raw honey
- 2 teaspoons pure vanilla extract

Balsamic Strawberries:
- 1 tablespoon almond butter
- 2 cups fresh strawberries, hulled and halved
- 1/4 cup raw honey
- 1 tablespoon balsamic vinegar

Directions
- **Pour** the coconut milk, 1/2 cup honey, and vanilla in a blender. Cover and blend on high until smooth and frothy. Pour mixture into a frozen ice cream bowl.

- **Cover**, and start ice cream maker to churn it. Transfer to a freezer safe container and freeze until serving.
- **Melt** almond butter in a large skillet over medium heat.
- **Stir** in the strawberries, honey, and balsamic vinegar, cook until heated through.
- **Place** scoops of the coconut vanilla ice cream into dessert bowls then top with the balsamic strawberries to serve.

71. Choco Hazelnut Biscotti

Servings: 6
Preparation time: 20 minutes
Cook time: 30 minutes
Ready in: 50 minutes

Nutrition Facts

Serving Size 81 g

Amount Per Serving

Calories 292   Calories from Fat 142

	% Daily Value*
Total Fat 15.8g	**24%**
Saturated Fat 2.9g	**15%**
Cholesterol 0mg	**0%**
Sodium 179mg	**7%**
Total Carbohydrates 36.9g	**12%**
Dietary Fiber 3.9g	**15%**
Sugars 28.9g	
Protein 6.4g	

Vitamin A 0%	•	Vitamin C 1%
Calcium 1%	•	Iron 6%

Nutrition Grade C-
* Based on a 2000 calorie diet

Ingredients
- 1 cup blanched almond flour
- 1/4 cup unsweetened cocoa powder
- 1/4 cup coconut flour
- 1/2 teaspoon baking soda
- 1/4 teaspoon unrefined sea salt
- 1/2 cup raw honey
- 1/2 cup hazelnuts, skinned and toasted
- 1/2 cup dark chocolate chips, coarsely chopped (70%-90% cocoa)

Directions
- **Preheat** oven to 350 degrees f. Line a baking sheet with parchment paper.
- **Place** almond flour, cocoa powder, coconut flour, baking soda, and salt in a food processor and pulse to combine. Stir in honey and pulse again.
- **Transfer** the dough into a bowl and stir in the hazelnuts and chocolate chips.
- **Shape** the dough into a log and place onto the baking sheet. **Bake** for 15 minutes. Let cool and cut the dough log into 1/2 inch thick slices on the diagonal using a bread knife.
- **Place** the slices cut side down on a parchment-lined baking sheet and return to the oven.
- **Bake** for 15 minutes at 250 degrees F. Let cool and serve.

72. Holiday Fruit Cake

Servings: 8
Preparation time: 15 minutes
Cook time: 20-30 minutes
Ready in: 35 minutes

Nutrition Facts

Serving Size 140 g

Amount Per Serving	
Calories 351	Calories from Fat 264

	% Daily Value*
Total Fat 29.3g	**45%**
Saturated Fat 2.8g	**14%**
Trans Fat 0.0g	
Cholesterol 0mg	**0%**
Sodium 178mg	**7%**
Total Carbohydrates 17.3g	**6%**
Dietary Fiber 4.6g	**18%**
Sugars 10.2g	
Protein 8.3g	

Vitamin A 4%	•	Vitamin C 5%
Calcium 5%	•	Iron 9%

Nutrition Grade D+
* Based on a 2000 calorie diet

Ingredients
- 1 1/2 cups hazelnut flour
- 1/2 teaspoon baking soda

- 1/2 teaspoon unrefined sea salt
- 1 cup pecans, chopped
- 1/2 cup dried cranberries, chopped
- 1/2 cup raisins
- 1/2 cup dried apricots, chopped
- 4 pasture-fed, free-range eggs
- 2 tablespoons grape seed oil
- 1 tablespoon raw honey
- 1 tablespoon pure vanilla extract
- 1/2 tablespoon ground cinnamon
- Coconut oil for greasing

Directions

- **Preheat** oven to 350°f. Grease 2 mini loaf pans with coconut oil.
- **Mix** the hazelnut flour, baking soda, and salt in a large bowl. Add the pecans and dried fruits.
- **Whisk** together the eggs, grape seed oil, honey, vanilla, and cinnamon in another bowl. Pour egg mixture over the flour mixture then stir well to combine.
- **Pour** batter into the loaf pans.
- **Bake** fruitcakes for 20-30 minutes. Let cool, slice, and serve.

73. Coconut Almond Macaroons

Servings: 6
Preparation time: 45 minutes
Cook time: 10-12 minutes
Ready in: 55 minutes

Nutrition Facts	
Serving Size 156 g	
Amount Per Serving	
Calories 335	Calories from Fat 203
	% Daily Value*
Total Fat 22.5g	**35%**
Saturated Fat 13.3g	**66%**
Trans Fat 0.0g	
Cholesterol 0mg	**0%**
Sodium 63mg	**3%**
Total Carbohydrates 30.9g	**10%**
Dietary Fiber 6.7g	**27%**
Sugars 17.6g	
Protein 7.4g	
Vitamin A 0% • Vitamin C 0%	
Calcium 5% • Iron 4%	
Nutrition Grade D-	
* Based on a 2000 calorie diet	

Ingredients
- 2 large egg whites
- 2 1/2 cups unsweetened coconut flakes
- 1/2 cup roasted almond nuts, chopped
- 1/4 cup raw honey
- 1/2 teaspoon pure vanilla extract
- 1/2 teaspoon ground cinnamon
- 1/4 teaspoon unrefined sea salt
- 1 cup cold water

Directions
- **Preheat** oven to 350 degrees f. Line a baking sheet with parchment paper.
- **Whisk** together the egg whites, coconut flakes, and almonds in a bowl. Stir in honey, vanilla, cinnamon, and salt. Chill the batter for 30 minutes.

- **Stir** the batter a few times. Scoop out batter (about 2 tablespoons for each macaroon) and dip in cold water. Place ball into the baking sheet.
- **Bake** the macaroons for 10 minutes, or until golden brown. Cool and serve.

74. Cinnamon Apple Crisps

Servings: 8
Preparation time: 10 minutes
Cook time: 45 minutes
Total time: 55 minutes

Nutrition Facts

Serving Size 244 g

Amount Per Serving	
Calories 139	Calories from Fat 4
	% Daily Value*
Total Fat 0.4g	**1%**
Trans Fat 0.0g	
Cholesterol 0mg	**0%**
Sodium 3mg	**0%**
Total Carbohydrates 36.8g	**12%**
Dietary Fiber 7.3g	**29%**
Sugars 26.0g	
Protein 0.3g	

Vitamin A 3%	•	Vitamin C 30%
Calcium 4%	•	Iron 3%

Nutrition Grade A
* Based on a 2000 calorie diet

Ingredients
- 6 large apples, juiced (about 2 cups)
- 1 cinnamon stick
- 2 large apples
- 2 lemons, juiced
- 1 tablespoon raw honey
- 2 tablespoons ground cinnamon
- 1 tablespoon ground nutmeg

Directions
- **Place** a large pot over high heat. Add apple juice and cinnamon stick; bring to a low boil. Using a knife, chop off

161

top and bottom of apples. Slice crosswise into thin chips; remove any seeds.

- **Sprinkle** apple chips with lemon juice and honey. Drop the apple slices into boiling juice and cook for 4-5 minutes, or until translucent.
- **Preheat** oven to 250°F.
- **Remove** apple slices from juice and dry them on a cloth towel. Place a wire cooling rack on a baking sheet. Spread out the slices on the rack and sprinkle with cinnamon and nutmeg.
- **Bake** for 30-40 minutes until crispy.

Books by Andrea Huffington

Paleo Slow Cooker Recipes

The Easy Paleo Diet Beginner's Guide

Going Paleo on a Budget

www.amazon.com/author/andrea-huffington

About Andrea Huffington

Andrea Huffington is an author, professional speaker and health coach extraordinaire.

Growing up in Southern California, Andrea has struggled with being overweight since early childhood. After completing a degree in chemical engineering at UCLA (where she also met her husband James), she took an internship in India. Shortly thereafter she had to return to the United States to receive treatment for her progressively worsening diabetes. After this health scare and trying various different diets and approaches, she found the Paleo way of eating and has never looked back. Today she is a picture of health and wellness, and participates in triathlons and frequently gives talks on the subject of how the Paleo diet impacts sports fitness and emotional health.

She believes that in keeping things simple we can achieve so much more. This has certainly worked for her!

Recently Andrea has spent three months with the San people of the Kalahari Desert in a quest to discover the secrets of their endurance and stamina in hot desert conditions.

Andrea lives in Hawaii with her husband, three children, two dogs and a pet Boa Constrictor.

One Last Thing...

Thank you so much for reading my book. I hope you really liked it. As you probably know, many people look at the reviews on Amazon before they decide to purchase a book. If you liked the book, could you please take a minute to leave a review with your feedback? 60 seconds is all I'm asking for, and it would mean the world to me.

Andrea Huffington

NaturalWay
Publishing

Atlanta, Georgia USA

25046443R00093

Made in the USA
Lexington, KY
12 August 2013